MEMOIRS
OF THE HARVARD DEAD
IN THE WAR
AGAINST GERMANY

I
THE VANGUARD

MEMOIRS
OF THE HARVARD DEAD
IN THE WAR
AGAINST GERMANY

By M. A. DeWOLFE HOWE

VOLUME I

CAMBRIDGE
HARVARD UNIVERSITY PRESS
MCMXX

PREFACE

Under appointment by the President and Fellows of Harvard College, the "Biographer of the Harvard Dead in the War against Germany" is preparing a series of memoirs of the men whose names are inscribed on the Harvard Roll of Honor. This list, now exceeding three hundred and sixty in number, is made up of all those, ever enrolled as students or officers of Harvard University, who, as members of the fighting and auxiliary forces of the United States and the Allied Powers in the European War, have given their lives in service, or in direct consequence of that service, provided their deaths occur before the signing of peace between the United States and the Central Powers.

The Harvard War Records Office and the collections of the Harvard Memorial Society have provided much material for these memoirs. Still more has been secured through direct correspondence with the families of the "Harvard Dead." Many parents and friends have been most liberal in the lending of letters, diaries, and other memorials. For all this kindness I would express here a warm appreciation.

There has deliberately been no attempt to "standardize" the memoirs with respect either to length or to character. It has seemed better simply to make in each instance what could be made, within reasonable bounds, of the material at hand. Every effort has been put forth to secure equal supplies of material from all sources, but without success. This will explain in some measure the varying lengths of the memoirs that follow.

PREFACE

In this first volume of "Memoirs of the Harvard Dead" only those thirty men are included whose deaths occurred before the United States entered the European War, April 6, 1917. They were "The Vanguard," the men who sealed with their blood the pledge of that overwhelming sentiment in favor of the Allies which in time was to make our country an active participant in the fight. They deserve a volume to themselves. Those who give their all before anything is asked must be held in separate remembrance and gratitude.

Throughout the work it is purposed to take up the subjects, as in this volume, in the chronological sequence of their deaths.

M. A. DeW. H.

Boston, *March, 1920.*

CONTENTS

CONTENTS

MEMOIRS

Ah, young heroes, safe in immortal youth as those of Homer, you at least carried your ideal hence untarnished. It is locked for you beyond moth or rust in the treasure-chamber of Death.

JAMES RUSSELL LOWELL

GEORGE WILLIAMSON

Class of 1905

George Williamson, the first graduate of Harvard to give his life in the war, is said also to have been the first graduate of any American college so to have fallen. He was born in London, September 26, 1883, the son of Charles James and Martha Lauretta (Long) Williamson. His mother is now Lady Skinner, the wife of Sir Thomas Skinner, of Montreal, a director of the Canadian Pacific Railway. The boy's preparation for college was made at St. Paul's School, Concord, New Hampshire. His college friends, for whom a classmate has spoken, recall him as virile, witty, of good habits, exceptionally liked, and brilliant enough to maintain a good academic standing without much study. The mere fact that at the sophomore dinner of his class he responded to the toast of "The Grind" suggests that he was not too hard a student: after-dinner speeches of this kind are generally assigned on the *lucus a non lucendo* principle. Williamson's college interests are further indicated by the fact that he was a member of the Institute of 1770, the Polo, Hasty Pudding, and Fly Clubs, and the editorial staff of the *Harvard Advocate*. In the sketches — they were hardly stories — which he contributed to that journal, the English background of the young editor provided a refreshing bit of contrast with the familiar stock-in-trade of our college journalism. Read even today his contributions to the *Advocate* have qualities both of poise and of liveliness to which one responds with genuine liking.

Graduating at Harvard in 1905, Williamson went at once to England where he matriculated at Oxford University, in October, as a member of Christ Church. While at Oxford he joined the Duke of Wellington's West Riding Regiment, of which he was a lieutenant in the Third Reserve Battalion. He became a student of the Inner Temple in 1906, and left Oxford at Easter, 1907. In January, 1910, he was admitted to the bar, and on November 9, 1910, married Hilda Isabel Gordon of Montreal, where he entered upon the practice of his profession. When the war came, four years later, he was a member of the Montreal law firm of Smith, Markey, Skinner, Pugsley, and Hyde.

Early in August he was summoned by cable to join his regiment, and proceeded at once to England. The first battalion of the regiment was in India; the second had already gone to France. After about two weeks of training with his own, the Third Reserve Battalion, Williamson left England for the front, September 8. The retreat from Mons had ended, and the Allies had resumed the offensive. Of what befell him from that time forth there is no occasion to resort to other words than those of a private letter [1] which formed the basis of a sketch of Williamson's military service in the *Harvard Graduates' Magazine* for March, 1915:

George went through the battles on the Aisne and on the Marne, and wrote several very cheery letters to his family at this time. Officers of his battalion who have since come home, including his captain, bear testimony to his splendid behaviour during this trying time when they were constantly under shell-fire, and he apparently was exactly the same as ever, cracking jokes and cheering his men by his bearing.

When the regiment arrived on the present lines, George, according to his captain, who has since also been wounded and come home, greatly distinguished himself on one occasion when the trench his section were holding was attacked by the bayonet, and George's lot succeeded in throwing back the enemy after desperate hand-to-hand fighting.

On November 8, George's company advanced in the early morning to relieve the defenders of a certain trench. George's section were on the left of the company and advanced along the outside edge of a wood. The enemy had worked around further to the left and opened fire with machine guns, enfilading George's men. These latter took cover in the wood as fast as they could, and George might easily have saved himself by doing the same. Instead, however, he stepped out of the wood and took a good look round to make certain that all his men had got safely to cover, and thereupon was hit five times all down the left side, including one in the lung. He kept going, however, long enough to get his men safely into the trench, and then actually walked along it to the centre and reported himself wounded to the captain.

[1] Written December 17, 1914, by Edward Bell, '04.

He had to sit till nightfall in the trench, and then was moved seventeen miles in a motor ambulance to a hospital [at Poperinghe]. He and the doctors all thought he would recover and he wrote on the 10th to his mother giving the date of his probable arrival in England, and making light of his wounds. On the night of the 11th he grew rapidly worse and died early the following morning. He was buried nearby and his grave is marked.

His wife, and their one child, Hazel, born August 12, 1911, made all haste to reach Europe from Montreal when the news of his wounds came to them there, but were still on the ocean when he died.

EDWARD MANDELL STONE

CLASS OF 1908

THE first Harvard man to die in the war was completely English; the second was completely American. He was Edward Mandell Stone, born January 5, 1888, at Chicago, Ill., the third son of Henry Baldwin Stone, of the Harvard Class of 1873, and Elizabeth Mandell Stone, both natives of New Bedford, Massachusetts. Henry Baldwin Stone had made for himself a typically American career: on graduation he began work as a machinist in a Waltham cotton mill; then he went West, and entered the shops of the Chicago, Burlington and Quincy Railroad at Aurora, Ill.; in a few years he became general manager of the Burlington system and second vice-president of the road. Later he was made president of the Chicago Telephone Company and of two other companies representing the great interests of the Bell Telephone system in the central states, a position which he held until a few days before his death. This occurred, July 5, 1897, through an accident. His wife died in 1907.

Their son, Edward, who made his home in Milton, with his mother until her death, and then with his sister, was prepared for college at Milton Academy, and entered Harvard with the Class of 1908. He completed his work for the A.B. degree in 1907, and during his senior year studied in the Law School. He did not finish his studies there, but in 1909 served in the Legation at Buenos Aires as a volunteer private secretary to the Hon. Charles H. Sherrill, United States Minister to the Argentine Republic. Returning to this country he entered the Graduate School of Arts and Sciences in January, 1910, taking courses in history and political science, and the next autumn resumed his course in the Law School. His graduate work showed marked intelligence and a capability which would have carried him far had he taken up the practice of the law. Of the man himself Mr. Sherrill, speaking of his first interview with Stone upon his arrival in South America, has written:

> He was excessively modest, frankly avowing that he had no delusions as to his mental equipment for making a great success of his life, but in that interview and throughout my subsequent relations with him there always appeared an unswerving integrity of purpose, and a desire to be helpful. Those are the traits which seemed most to mark his character, and those are the traits which later led him to make his life more useful to civilization than our lives will probably be.

This first Harvard volunteer to die for France bore a relation to the war of which there is little to tell beyond a record of his service. Reserved and chary of expression, he was averse equally from letting himself be photographed and from writing about himself in his infrequent letters. He had been living in France for some time before the outbreak of the war, and had become deeply interested in this country and fond of its people. When Germany attacked France in August, 1914, he enlisted at once as a private in the Foreign Legion, 2nd Regiment, Battalion C. In October he was sent to the trenches at the front with a machine-gun section, and served at or near Craonne until wounded there by shrapnel on February 15, 1915. He was taken to the Military Hospital at Romilly, where he died of his wounds on February 27, 1915. He is buried in the Military Cemetery of Romilly. His family have felt sure that his own wish would have been to lie in the country which he loved and served.

His class secretary reports of him that when he received his fatal wound a surgeon asked if he wished him to write to anybody, but that Stone said it was not worth while. "These words are, in a way, characteristic of the man. What he did he did well, and invariably felt that no particular attention should be paid to the results he achieved. He was an essentially modest person who took life as he found it, and contributed to everything he took part in both with high ideals and straightforward work."

The surgeon of the Foreign Legion who first cared for him after his wound has written:

I saw Eddie Stone frequently during the six months we were together in "*Bataillon C, 2ème Régiment de marche du 2ème Étrangère.*" He was always on the job and in good spirits: he had a lot of grit, poor chap.

One day I got a call from his company to treat a wounded man. It was Stone, I found, with a hole in his side made by a shrapnel ball, which had probably penetrated his left lung. There was no wound of exit, so the ball, or piece of shell, stayed in. He was carried back by my squad of stretcher-bearers from the front line trench — the "*Blanc Sablon*," our headquarters — where I had applied the first dressing, and from there removed to a hospital about eight miles back. I did not see him again, and heard that he died of his wound in this hospital.

He had friends in the Legion who spoke highly of him to me. There was very little help we regimental doctors could give the wounded, I am sorry to say. All we could do for them was to see that they were carefully moved back out of the firing zone after a first dressing. You can tell his people that he always did his duty as a soldier and died like one. Of this I am sure.

ANDRÉ CHÉRONNET-CHAMPOLLION

CLASS OF 1902

It is a true symbol of the diversity of the Harvard fellowship and of the common interests of England, America, and France that, following an Englishman and an American, the third Harvard man to fall in the war was a native of France, André Chéronnet-Champollion, born in Paris, September 20, 1880. In 1904, two years after his graduation at Harvard, he became an American citizen. His mother was an American, a daughter of the late Austin Corbin, president of the Long Island Railroad, a man of affairs whose interest in nature expressed itself, through the later years of his life, in the maintenance of buffalo and other American animals in his forest and game preserve at Newport, New Hampshire. This American grandfather had an interesting counterpart in Champollion's French great-grandfather, Jean François Champollion, "Champollion the Younger," whose deciphering of the hieroglyphics of the Rosetta stone made him the founder of modern Egyptology. Before his death in 1832, handing his unpublished "*Grammaire Égyptienne*" to his older brother, also a distinguished orientalist, he said, "*Voilà, j'espère, ma carte de visite à la posterité.*" His great-grandson, as the first Harvard man of French descent to die in the war, has strengthened the hold of his name upon the generations still to come.

It is not surprising that André Chéronnet-Champollion's blended inheritances should have made him an unusual person. While he was still a boy in France his father died, and several years later, his mother. Thereupon, at the age of twelve, he came to America, to be brought up by his maternal grandparents. From their home in New York he went to St. Paul's School, Concord, and afterwards to Harvard College. Here he made a creditable record, and in his senior year was not only president of the Cercle Français but took part in its presentation of Racine's "*Les Plaideurs.*" He was a member, also, of the Institute of 1770, the Hasty Pudding, and Zeta Psi. It was after college that his distinctive tastes and characteristics became clearly manifest. For the tenth annual report of his class he wrote:

After leaving college I took a trip around the world, stopping to hunt in Alaska. I visited Japan, China, the Philippines, the Malay States, Ceylon, India, Burma, and Egypt. I had intended to become a portrait painter, but on seeing India I became so enthusiastic about that country that I decided to make it the subject of future paintings. On returning I studied four years at the

Art Students' League in New York, taking another trip to India in the fall and winter of 1908–09. In the spring of 1909 I travelled through Manchuria, visiting the scenes of the Russo-Japanese war; I returned by way of Siberia and Russia. In the fall of 1912, after three years more of study, I shall return to India for six months, after which I expect to begin exhibiting. Later on I hope to include Mexico and old Japan as subjects for paintings. I am a great admirer of the Russian painter Verestchagin. My favorite recreation is big game hunting. I have shot grizzly bears in Alaska, moose and deer in New Brunswick, caribou and black bear in Newfoundland, besides elk, deer, and wild bear on a private game preserve. I have hunted tigers in China, but without success.

In this report he noted that he had contributed an article on "Hunting the Alaskan Grizzly" to *Forest and Stream.* It is also recorded that in 1908 he married Adelaide Strong Knox, a daughter of the late John Jay Knox, of New York, Comptroller of the Currency of the United States. Their only son, René, was born in 1909.

It is not related in Champollion's report of himself that while he was making his trip round the world the Russo-Japanese War began, or that his admiration of the painter Verestchagin was joined with a desire to become, as Champollion's friend, Anton Schefer, has expressed it, "a painter of the same type, one who should depict the horrors of warfare with intense realism, in order to further the cause of peace."

When the war broke out, Champollion, who had recently secured his final release from all military obligation in France, was living in Newport, New Hampshire. He saw immediately that, in spite of all the rights and inclinations which made for his remaining in America, his place was in

France, and in the fight. His gravest misgivings were on the score of his duty to his wife and child. His wide experience of life in the open had given him one excellent qualification for soldiering, though this may well have been offset by the sensitiveness to suffering and ugliness that was part of his endowment as an artist. Yet none of these considerations held him, and before the middle of October, 1914, he was a private in the French Army, serving at Sens (Yonne) in a platoon of candidates for promotion.

Here, from October till the end of February, 1915, he drilled as a private, hoping to be made an interpreter if not to win a commission, receiving neither of these rewards, refusing to be made a corporal or sergeant, because he valued the private's leisure, and because, as he wrote in a letter, "to be a successful corporal or sergeant, you have to get into the habit of abusing men who cannot answer back, and that is contrary to all my principles of sportsmanship." It was a period of much discouragement and depression, at one time almost of a nervous breakdown. Mrs. Champollion came from America, and established herself in an apartment in Sens, where her husband could be much with her. This saved the day, and when Champollion went to the front late in February, still a private, his letters revealed a spirit far better satisfied than it had been. A friend in New York, Anton Schefer, of the class after his own at Harvard, has made a privately printed volume of these letters to friends—("Letters from André Chéronnet-Champollion, 1914–1915") — a poignant and distinctive memorial. A succession of passages, taken here and there from its pages, will permit Champollion to speak for himself:

SENS, *October 14, 1914.* It looks as if the war was going to last many months. . . . I left America with the understanding that I should be back there in time for Easter Sunday, but it looks now as if I should have to wait for the next football season.

November 12. Most of the men here to whom I have related the story of my life and the forces that drove me here, evince statements of puzzled curiosity as to how any one with as good excuses as mine for staying away could voluntarily have plunged himself into an ocean of trouble. . . . I feel so totally out of place amid such surroundings, for the other men are most of them young peasant chaps, that I have terrible moments of doubt. I often feel like a fool instead of like an honest man trying to do his duty. . . . I often wonder if I will ever come back to see René grow up, to be his first guide in the Park, and to watch his progress through St. Paul's School and Harvard. When I compare my attractive New Hampshire home to the terrible gloom of the barracks and cantonments, and I see the Park in all its splendor and loveliness, even New York, which I used to curse at a good deal, now seems like a paradise that is out of reach. Never has America seemed so beautiful.

December 3. You cannot help wondering now and then what effect such a stagnating existence is going to have on your mind, supposing you get out of it alive and unhurt. Must fifteen years of study and ten years of hard work on art result in your dying at the age of thirty-four of intellectual dry rot? I had imagined war more painful physically, but not nearly so morally. . . . At all events I still persist in the belief that I should always have had a most uncomfortable feeling of shame and of duty undone if I had remained in America.

January 17, 1915. The trouble with the whole continent of Europe is that to them the word "Sport" is unknown. To them it is a frivolous way of spending one's time. If the Germans had been sportsmen and had not taken themselves so infernally seriously, they would have been incapable of the atrocities they are accused of. No sportsman, no nation of sportsmen, would be capable of the things they are reported to have done as reprisals for very small offences. The Frenchman either takes life too seriously or too frivolously. He is either a grind or a loafer (a gentleman of leisure). Who ever heard of a member of the French Academy being a good golfer, or of a French bishop playing a good game of tennis, of a French president being distinguished in any branch of sport ! And this spirit permeates the whole military system of this country. The trouble with Europe is that there is not enough football, tennis, golf, or base-ball. This sounds very frivolous, but it is a sincere conviction now. The whole damned continent needs new life, new ideas, new everything. Let all those who are Americans thank their stars that they are no longer members of the morbid European nations. It is as bad for nations as for individuals to take themselves too seriously and not get out of doors and play ball once in a while. I believe if they had, this war might never have taken place.

January 30. I frankly confess that if Adelaide had not arrived I would have broken down entirely. Her arrival was to me like a life preserver to a drowning man.

Less than a month before Champollion was ordered to the front he was still hoping for a favorable response to his application for appointment as an interpreter. "If it does not succeed," he wrote, "I shall go and take my medicine like the rest, I suppose, and for months lead the life of a woodchuck whose hole is within fifty yards of the house of a farmer who is a dead shot with a rifle!" This life he was destined to lead for less than a month. He reached the front at the end of February. On March 1 he wrote a vivid letter in which he said, "I have indicated by a star every time a shell passes over us during the composition of this note. If I punctuated the explosions I should have to stop between letters." The printed page shows a terribly significant sprinkling of asterisks. A few other letters followed — courageous, clear-sighted, blindingly illuminating. On March 23, 1915, the end came. Lieutenant Lucien Courtois, of Champollion's regiment of the French Army, wrote of it, and of him, as follows:

I quickly learned to sympathize with him, because I saw him to be rather strange in surroundings altogether new to him, and because I admired deeply the beauty of his action, which had made him forget his interests and affections, to come, spontaneously, to France in danger. We often talked together. I saw him accomplish his daily duties as a soldier in the trenches with constant modesty, good humor, sang-froid, and great indifference to danger, and this sympathy changed soon to profound friendship.

He was struck by a bullet in the forehead, on the 23rd of March, when the Germans, having unexpectedly exploded a mine in one of our trenches, attempted to invade our lines. To check them as quickly as possible, our company was making a barricade of sacks of earth to fill the breach. It was when coöperating in this work, with his habitual courage that he was struck.

He was buried in the cemetery of Petan, near the village of Montauville, at the entrance of the Bois-le-Prêtre, where his regiment, the 168th of the Line, had been fighting all winter. He was awarded the *Croix de Guerre* and cited for bravery in the Army order of the day for July 15, 1917, reading as follows:

128E DIVISION, 168E RÉGIMENT D'INFANTERIE.
ORDRE DU RÉGIMENT NO. 90.

Citation, — Le Lt.-Colonel Cdt. le 168e Régiment d'Infanterie cite à l'Ordre du Régiment le Brave dont le nom suit:

Chéronnet-Champollion, André; 2 classe, 4 compagnie.

A quitté les États-Unis, où il était établi, pour venir dès la déclaration de guerre prendre sa place sur le front. Soldat courageux et brave. Le 23 Mars, 1915, au Bois-le-Prêtre, s'est offert comme volontaire pour réparer sous le feu, sa tranchée qui venait d'être bouleversée par l'explosion souterraine d'un fourneau de mine allemand. A été tué d'une balle en plein front au moment où il accomplissait sa mission avec le plus absolu mépris du danger.

CHEPY,
Le Lt.-Col., Cdt. le 168e R. I.

LE 24 JUILLET 1917.

HAROLD MARION-CRAWFORD

CLASS OF 1911

THIS son of Francis Marion Crawford and Elizabeth (Berdan) Crawford was born in Sorrento, Italy, February 1, 1888. His father, the well-known novelist, was the son of Thomas Crawford, the sculptor, whose wife, afterwards Mrs. Terry, a sister of Mrs. Julia Ward Howe, was a familiar figure in Roman society. An eighteenth century ancestor, whose name the novelist bore, was General Francis Marion, the "Swamp Fox" of Revolutionary fame. The father of Mrs. Francis Marion Crawford was Hiram Berdan, colonel of the first regiment of the United States Sharpshooters in the Civil War, brevetted major-general for his conduct at Gettysburg, inventor of a rifle and other devices of military and naval warfare. Harold Marion-

Crawford had thus a strongly marked American background of descent, though his birth in Italy and his preparation for college under a tutor in England, and then, for a short time, in Cambridge, brought him to Harvard by steps not at all characteristic of the American boy. His career in College, which he entered in the autumn of 1907, with the Class of 1911, was no more typical, for he did not complete even his freshman year. Nor was his next recorded step in any conventional direction since it bore him to the Federated Malay States in the employ of the English rubber-planting firm, the Luiggi Plantations, Ltd. Here, by 1910, he was a sub-manager, and later was made manager of a Division of the Plantations. In 1911 he married, in Singapore, Nina Noreen Wood, only daughter of the late C. W. Wood, Esq., R. N., of Dublin, and the late Nina de Burgh (Egan) Wood. In 1913 he came to England, his wife's home, for a year's leave. There, on January 17, 1914, their only son, Howard Francis Marion-Crawford, was born.

He had planned to return to the East at about the middle of August, and would have done so but for the declaration of war. Instead, he immediately obtained a commission in the Irish Guards, which he held for nearly six months. He was then made Bomb Officer to the 4th Guards Brigade, a post which involved the constant handling of explosives, many of them in an experimental stage. A few bits from his letters from the front reveal the conditions of his daily life.

January 7, 1915. We are just leaving for the firing line again after a few days well earned rest. Since I wrote you, we had a most appalling time in the trenches; what with the water, mud, and fighting, hell could never compare with it. It is hard to find any news from here without going into details which one is not allowed to give, but it is all so vividly impressed on my mind that I believe I can tell you what happened day by day when I get back. I am very well and stronger than anybody, but this is a very depressing country and I can't help getting depressed sometimes. We all long for HOME, and heartily wish it were all over!

January 21, 1915. We are having another short rest which we all greatly appreciate. The trenches are too appalling for words! The last we were in were waist deep in running water and mud! Standing in this sort of stuff for days and nights on end is really the most terrific strain on one's system that could possibly be imagined. The extraordinary thing about it is that I am as fit as a fiddle, very thin, and in the best of spirits. This war, I am sure, is the most wonderful war that anyone has ever dreamt of. The fighting consists of sitting in a trench and firing at one another when anybody pops up his head; bar this, they shell us occasionally, which is very unpleasant and that is all. The mud and water are our worst enemies and quite bad enough, too.

February 24, 1915. I have been in every second of the fighting you have read of in the papers lately. My C.O. recommended me for a "ribbon and a bit of tin of sorts," but if I get anything or not remains to be seen.

After this duty he came home from France on leave, April 4, 1915, and returned April 11. On April 16, while he was giving an explanatory lecture at Givenchy to a party from the Coldstream Guards, a hand grenade exploded, killing him on the spot.

His colonel testified to the reality of his loss "both as an officer and a comrade." A younger brother-officer wrote with more intimacy of personal knowledge: "A great loss to the Irish Guards, but much more to us and his company who knew him so well. Great-hearted and loved by all, full of life and confidence, I only wish he was with us instead of lying buried behind Givenchy, his grave covered with flowers by our sergeants who did their best to show how much he was to them."

CALVIN WELLINGTON DAY

GRADUATE SCHOOL, 1912–14

IN the long roll of the Harvard dead there are many names which Harvard is proud to share with other institutions of learning — the names of men whose connection with the University has been through membership in the graduate schools. With no abatement of allegiance to an earlier *alma mater*, these men find in Harvard a second mother to whom they often bring a beautiful devotion. The first Harvard man of this considerable class who fell in the war against Germany was Calvin Wellington Day, of Kingston, Ontario, a student in the Graduate School of Arts and Sciences from 1912 to 1914.

Born of United Empire Loyalist descent in Kingston, Ontario, April 19, 1891, the son of Sidney Wellington Day and Adelaide Isabella (Waggoner) Day of that city, Calvin Wellington Day had his schooling at the public schools and Collegiate Institute of Kingston and the Collegiate Institute of the town of Cobourg in the same province. He then became a student in Queen's University, Kingston, where he received the degree of A.M. in 1911, with first class honors in the physics and mathematics course and the University Medal in Physics. In 1911–12 he was assistant in physics in Queen's University. In the autumn of 1912 he entered the Graduate School of Arts and Sciences at Harvard for further studies in physics, and for the year 1913–14 held a Whiting Fellowship and served, though without formal appointment, as a research assistant.

The diary which he kept through his final weeks at Cambridge and thenceforward until within a few days of his death, and the letters to his family for virtually the same period, tell the story of his connection with the war and picture the man himself. A few extracts from both these sources must briefly serve the same double purpose. The first of the Cambridge entries describes his passing the last of his preliminary examinations for the Ph.D. degree:

All of the members of the division were present and they kept me up and bombarded me with questions for three hours. . . . When I came out I was nearly "all in," but when Professor Hall came out and told me that I had passed and seemed amused at my anxiety I revived somewhat. I celebrated by going to bed early that night.

The following pages of the diary touch upon the June and July pleasures of Cambridge, and the progress of some work Day was completing in the Physical Laboratory. There were good times at tennis and in other ways with girls of Cambridge and the Summer School. Class Day came and went: "I did n't believe that a place could change so quickly as did Harvard Square after Class Day. The Yard was like a vase with the flowers removed, yet beautiful withal."

Before the end of July there are notes about the political disturbance of Europe. As a schoolboy of sixteen at Cobourg, Day had joined the Cobourg Garrison Artillery, and at one of its summer camps had won the first prize for gun-laying and range-finding. In 1911 he had joined the Princess of Wales's Own Rifles (14th Regiment) at Kingston, and received his lieutenant's commission, April 3, 1912. As soon as it looked as if England might be involved in the impending conflict, Day therefore telegraphed to a major of his regiment, volunteering in case of need, and received a prompt reply saying that his message had been forwarded to Ottawa with recommendation. A piece of apparatus he was installing in the laboratory is set down as "a beauty," and then, in a few days, comes the news that England had sent an ultimatum to Germany: "so packed my belongings quietly and went out to dinner at Dr. Trueblood's. The next morning [August 5] I started for home." On the 6th he was in Kingston, and from that time forward things moved rapidly.

Day and his fellow-soldiers were soon transferred from the "Home Guard" to the "Overseas Contingent," and on the 22d he left Kingston for the camp at Valcartier, Quebec. Within a few days of his arrival there he fell in with a Harvard sophomore — to be encountered at a later day still more strangely — and wrote in his journal: "I nearly collapsed with surprise when I saw Brokenshire whom I had left in Cambridge sitting on a fence at midnight when I went to send my telegram to Major Dawson. He was in kilts" — having joined the 5th Canadian Royal Highlanders as a private. At Valcartier, as later overseas, Day found all possible pleasure in human contacts, and here as there, joined heartily in the hard work which was to make his military unit the fighting force it became. The diary records all this process, and before the end of September he is found embarked in the ship *Cassandra,* one of a fleet of thirty-one transports guarded by six cruisers which bore the Second Battalion of the Canadian Expeditionary Force to England, actually the first Canadian soldiers to land there.

On Sunday, October 11, at sea, he noted with equal satisfaction "a splendid sermon" and the fact that he had not heard a single "patriotic oration" since war was declared. He wrote besides:

> The people with whom I have come in contact, particularly the men of the contingent, have gone into this thing coolly and calmly with the characteristic British attitude. From the thought that the men have gone into this undertaking independently, and perhaps more or less, as the case may be, actuated by ideals and acting on principles and not under the influence of a sentimental hysteria more or less mild, as would be aroused by

an emotional outburst, I get considerable satisfaction. Few men, if any, were actuated by any but the purest motives, and were not dragooned, compelled, or bluffed into this thing, and in being given the responsibility and opportunity of being a very junior officer of such men I get great satisfaction.

The voyage from Gaspé Bay in the St. Lawrence to Plymouth lasted from October 3 to 14. The beauty of England, the might of the Plymouth fortifications, the pride of being in the first colonial contingent to arrive, the newness of it all — a newness of 1914, expressed in such a sentence as "Just now we are having a band concert and the band is playing the popular Tommy Atkins song, 'It 's a long way to Tipperary'" — these and many other sharp impressions find their record in diary and letters. Drake and the Armada came inevitably to mind. After the Canadians had disembarked at Devonport, in Plymouth harbor, and proceeded to Bustard Camp on Salisbury Plain for their further period of training, Day wrote to his family: "The boys had been on shipboard closely confined for twenty-four days, and the 'Second Armada,' as the Plymouth people called it, was so unexpected that the people were very enthusiastic and excited."

The actual scene is thus preserved in the diary:

October 19. Bustard Camp, Salisbury.

Last night at 9.15 we fell in and marched on to the pier, leaving our home of twenty-four days. As modern sea-voyages go it was quite long in point of time. We made off from the pier at 10 P.M. and marched through the narrow, paved streets of the Navy Yard between the towering stone walls. The tramp, tramp, tramp sounded even above the singing. When we struck town I understood what "Merry England" meant. In spite of the lateness of the hour, the streets were crowded and every window as we passed had its occupants. The old women and the young girls crowded into the road, and the lucky fellows on the outer flanks kissed everyone they liked. Mother, father, and daughter would be standing there together, and a soldier would stop to shake hands with the old people, to talk to them and kiss the young daughter, and the parents would not think anything of it at all. There was laughing and singing everywhere. The old ladies kissed the boys and wished them a safe return, and our company, thanks to my watchful care perhaps, was more orderly than the others. We did n't allow any girls being brought into the ranks, nor did any of our men fall out of the ranks and walk along the street with girls (except——till I saw him). But apart from that there was no interference. They exchanged souvenirs and everybody was happy and good-natured, and as one very nice-appearing man to whom I was speaking said, in all the merriment there was n't an objectionable word or suggestion to be heard. Merry England!

For something more than three months Day's regiment underwent a rigorous training on Salisbury Plain. Yet there were intervals of relaxation, and England could sometimes be found still at play. Once when Day was riding alone to visit a flying school not far from Bustard Camp his horse balked at a steam tractor, was led across a bridge over the Avon — "a creek" — Day called it in writing home — "about fifteen yards wide," when, he proceeds:

I heard a hue and cry behind and a hare darted across the field by the road with about a hundred hounds and a dozen red-coated squires and about thirty officers in khaki in pursuit. The Master dashed by me with a whip in his right hand, a cigarette between his lips, and his horn and the reins in his left hand, going full gallop — but still as if he were stuck to the saddle — and his horse scarcely a bit wet. My horse must have had sporting blood away back, for he started off full tilt — and I let him go. I am afraid and ashamed to say that I stayed perhaps a little closer to his neck than most good riders would, but I stayed on. Anyhow I think they noticed my puttees and knew that I was only an infantry officer.

Another participation in English sport, while Day and a friend were enjoying a glimpse of London, has its amusing chronicle:

In the afternoon we (Mac and I) went to Prince's Club, of which we are honorary members, and had a fine time skating. I never saw so much good skating at one time before. Mac was Canadian champion figure skater for two years. There's always an old fogy in a club. We were going a little fast and he stopped us and asked if we were Canadians, etc., and said the ice was like Europe, and was all full of little Belgiums, and that they did n't violate one another's neutrality. We caught on and did n't need to be told any more. We had crossed his little "area." After a time Mac remarked to him that some others were waltzing about and infringing a bit, and the old gentleman remarked, "Yes, but they're good skaters." Mac was dumfounded. I nearly laughed out loud.

But the young Canadian was well disposed to like what he found in England — "Happy Day" the men of his battalion called him — and at the same time to remember all that he had left across the Atlantic. A family birthday seemed never to pass unnoticed. On November 14 it was worth his while to jot down in his diary an item, probably picked up in an English newspaper, "Harvard students 'rotten egg' the Lion of Brunswick" — a statue not at that time shielded by the Germanic Museum. On January 1 he wrote home: "Heard yesterday that Harvard trimmed Yale 36–0 in the new Yale Bowl on November 22. Such is fame!" His keen interest in everything must have made him the soldier that stands revealed in a letter written at Bristol, February 8, 1915, when on the very point of embarking for the continent:

> When they were cutting down the establishment of officers I was a little nervous, but as Curry said, "Eat, drink, and be merry, for tomorrow you may go to Tidworth." When the signalling office was cut off the establishment, as such, and when the Colonel stopped me and asked me if I would take charge of the signallers in addition to a platoon — and said, "Now will you stand by me? " and I said ,"Sure Mike," or words to that effect, I was so tickled I could scarcely stand at attention. . . . We have absolutely no idea when or where we are going; it may be India, Egypt, Bordeaux, or Le Havre, but probably the latter. But they can't make me mad by doing things that way. In fact I like it.

Eight days before his death in the second battle of Ypres, he wrote to his sister, April 15, 1915: "We're going to Y——. 'They can't make us mad that way.' We're all sick and tired of this inaction." The refusal to be made "mad" seems to have been a matter of principle with him. The rough experiences in billets in the neighborhood of Armentières and Lille, and later in Belgium might have shaken such a philosophy of life, but in his diary of March 25, he wrote: "Am beginning to like this game. I always have a happy faculty for liking things as they are and wishing them to continue." The journal may speak still more fully for him:

> *April 4. Easter Sunday.* Father's Birthday. Cold and windy with a sprinkling of rain in the morning. Church parade at 10 A.M. with Holy Communion. It was a very impressive service. I won't forget it soon. The communion rail was made of

scaling ladders which the engineers had devised and make for getting over barbed wire entanglements in an assault. A large number of the men took communion, considerably over 100. I took the communion also. The last time was in Salisbury Cathedral about two months ago.

April 14. About 5 P.M. I got a wheel from Hdqrs., and started over the sticky up-hill road to Cassel. It is eight kilometres, but I got there before six. The road winds about on its way up the hill, and as one rises the level surrounding country unfolds itself like a map. It is the first time I ever saw a level country from a height, and in this thickly populated and highly developed country it is a very striking sight. On the way up I passed an auto coming down the broad level *pavé*, and in it was General Foch reading his daily papers. To enter the town one has to pass through an old, covered gateway. Inside all the ground is paved. There was the usual square with the usual collection of motor transports. The town is old and quaint, streets at different levels and twisting about. Some very venerable looking buildings. I pushed my bike up to the highest point where there is a little park, an old château, and a wireless station. Here I was agreeably and intensely surprised. The only other soldier up there was Brokenshire, Harvard '16. I had n't seen him since we left England. It was very strange and pleasing to me. We sat in one of the stone bastions, very like those at Fresh Pond in Cambridge which I remember so well, overlooking the level plain three hundred feet below with its great straight roads losing themselves like endless white ribbons in the mist and gathering darkness — the road to Dunkerque and the sea and the road to Ypres and the British wedge, from which direction the occasional report of an extra heavy gun was heard indistinctly. Here we talked of Harvard and Cambridge, and the places and the girls we had known. It was a pleasing and impressive sight in the setting sun and a very pleasant experience, and I was very sorry to leave it to him.

The letters and diary continue almost to the time of Day's death. On April 19, his twenty-fourth birthday, he writes to his family of a "bathing parade" at a pond in the grounds of an Antwerp merchant's château: "We had a dandy swim and ran about the grounds and summer houses and caves and bridges in our bare feet like a company of fairies. I had a gorgeous time." On the 21st he wrote: "They're playing the game hard up here just now." The men were billeted in barns ready to move at short notice, with lively bombardments very close at hand. "It is my turn," the letter ended, "as company orderly officer today and it is tea-time, so I will have to close."

The short letter of the next day, April 22, ended with these words:

> Just now they are "*going right to it.*" There is a horse waiting for me outside and I am going where I can see more of the row. I am enclosing a handkerchief for Mother and some lace for Mabel [his sister]. I got them down in the village, saw them making the lace.

This letter he never posted. It was found, July 8, 1915, amongst some old papers by a fellow officer and forwarded to the address of "The Day Family" in Kingston. On the very day after it was written, April 23, he was killed in action near St. Julien, at the Battle of Langemarck in Belgium in the Second Battle of Ypres. This battle was infamous in history for the first use of asphyxiating gas by the German Army, and memorable for the valor of the Canadian troops of which Lieutenant Day was so typical an officer.

CARLTON THAYER BRODRICK

Class of 1908

Brodrick was one of the five Harvard men who lost their lives in the sinking of the *Lusitania*. The other four were Richard Rich Freeman, Jr., '09, Edwin William Friend, '08, Elbert Hubbard, '97, and Herbert Stuart Stone, '94. All these may be said to have met their deaths in the war against Germany; but Brodrick was the only one of them so identified with the war through his own activities that this series of memoirs must include one of him. His name stands first on the list of the more than twenty Harvard men who died during the course of the war, while associated with one of the great auxiliary services. His title to this place is found in the work he did under Mr. Herbert

C. Hoover in London, early in the war, for the Commission for Relief in Belgium.

Carlton Thayer Brodrick was born in Dorchester (Boston), Massachusetts, January 22, 1887, the son of Alfred Herbert Brodrick and Etta Louise (Redding) Brodrick. His boyhood was passed in Dorchester and in Newton, where he was a pupil first of the Hyde Grammar School and then of the Newton High School. Graduating there with high standing in 1904, he entered the Class of 1908 at Harvard College. His natural bent and abilities expressed themselves in the high standing he took in chemistry, mathematics, and geology. In his junior year he won a "Detur," and as a senior held a John Harvard Scholarship, a coveted honorary reward for the best academic work. His tastes and loyalties in College were suggested by his membership in the St. Paul's Society, the Sigma Alpha Epsilon, the Mining, Track and Field, and Chess Clubs. After graduating *cum laude*, he took up the higher study of mining, metallurgy, geology, and engineering in the Graduate School, and although he left the University before completing the work he had planned, received the degree of A.M. in 1910 with highest honors in geology.

Professor John E. Wolff has written of Brodrick at this time as "a very earnest, intelligent and enterprising student," and has added: "I call him enterprising because after taking the summer school of geology in Montana he spent part of another summer, alone or with a packer, in a rather remote part of the British Columbia mountains, working out the geology of a little known district, and this took a certain amount of courage and determination and initiative, unusual in one so young."

From the angle of a contemporary, his classmate and friend, Harold O. Wellman, wrote in the Newton *Graphic* of May 28, 1916:

Throughout his college course Brodrick showed a lively interest in mining geology, and during his summer vacations made many trips, both for the College and on his own account, to the Rocky Mountain regions, British Columbia, and other points in the Northwest.

His professors who guided his work even now speak of the energy and enthusiasm he manifested in making these researches, and of his constant interest in applying and working out in the field at every opportunity the theories studied in the classroom. Extraordinary facility in languages enabled Brodrick during these years to continue his engineering studies in the works of Russian, Swedish, and Italian authorities, as well as French and German, until in 1910, when he left his college courses to accept an appointment in the United States Geological Survey, he had a knowledge and grasp of his subject remarkably wide for a man of his years.

His work in the Government service at Washington early attracted the attention of Sidney H. Ball, the well-known mining engineer, who took Brodrick with him in the fall of that year to the Atbasar district in southwestern Siberia. There they remained six months, engaged in geological studies, particularly of copper occurrences, in which Brodrick's work proved so sound that he was engaged the next year as mining geologist by the Russo-Asiatic Company, controlling large mining interests in the Kyshtim district of the Ural Mountain region.

At that time the Russo-Asiatic Company was just at the beginning of its enormous development, and soon Brodrick, who was then only in his twenty-fourth year, was being sent all over Russia and Siberia to investigate new properties and report on their mining possibilities, a work which required the exercise, not only of expert knowledge, but also of sound and far-seeing judgment.

Signal success in this work led to further promotion, and in less than two years, Brodrick was advanced to the post of consulting geologist to the Russo-Asiatic Company. In this capacity he examined and reported upon a considerable number of important Russian and Siberian mining properties, of which the following have since become of notable interest: Tanalyk, Verkh, Issetsk, Miass, Sissert, and Revda. His latest work was an examination of the wonderful Ridder mining properties in western Siberia, which are generally regarded by mining experts as one of the four or five great mining developments of the decade.

To an engineer as young as Brodrick, it was no slight recognition of his judgment and ability on the part of the company that he should have been given the opportunity of being closely identified with the early development of a mining proposition of such magnitude and importance.

During these few years of rapid advancement and widening experience in his profession, Brodrick never lost active interest in his Alma Mater, and he made a practice of devoting a major part of the vacations spent in this country to the service of the Geological Museum of Harvard University. There he brought together specimens from foreign districts he had examined, and formed a large and valuable collection of Russian and Siberian ores, supplemented by an unusually complete fund of information gathered by him as to their occurrence in the field.

What all this meant to one of Brodrick's former teachers, the following words of Professor Wolff's will suggest:

As a young man active and successful in his profession as mining geologist he impressed me as thoroughly competent for the work he was doing, loyal to the interests he served, with a refreshing joy and whole-heartedness in his work. In his occasional visits home on leave from the great mining company in Siberia by which he was employed, he always visited the College and greeted his old associates and friends with unfailing friendship; he usually brought some interesting mineral specimens from Siberia and in other ways showed his attachment to the institution. He always made me a visit and it was a joy to talk with him, he was so full of delight in what he was doing, so happy with life, with glimpses of deep devotion to his family and friends; he was high-minded and clean. He was physically tall and active, no superfluous flesh, long-limbed.

It happened that Mr. Herbert C. Hoover was consulting engineer of the Russian mining companies for which Brodrick was working when the war broke out. On his way to America for his annual vacation he stopped in London, in January and February, 1915, and joined the force of Belgian Relief workers under Mr. Hoover there. Thence he proceeded to Boston where he spent two happy months with his family and friends. One of those who saw him at this time was Dr. D. W. Abercrombie of the Harvard Class of 1876, then principal of the Worcester Academy. On the sinking of the *Lusitania* he wrote to Brodrick's father, whom he had never seen, telling how he and the younger man, while still an undergraduate, had met in the White Mountains, and snow-shoed together:

Carlton [he went on] greatly interested me by his ingenuousness of mind and lovable spirit, and deep interest in things that were worth while. I felt very affectionately towards him, and called him one day my "papoose" because of his long, loping stride as we walked over the crunching snow. For many years he wrote me, and once he visited me. I tried to keep informed in regard to his growing capacity, for I was sure he was going to make a name for himself in the world. Within less than four weeks of his sailing, I think it was, I met him in Boston as he was taking a train for Cornell, and he and I were seat-mates as far as Worcester. He told me of his later experiences in Russia, and of his intended return on the first of May on the *Lusitania*. When that great ship went down by the dastardly act of the German government I thought instantly of Carlton, and looked with great anxiety on the lists of those saved and of those lost, and to my horror and sorrow, and grief that will never leave me, I saw that that splendid fellow had been lost. . . .

I can only tell you that I am one of those many men who loved Carlton and who foresaw for him a great career, and that I grieve not as you do but as a friend may for your son's early and terrible loss. I shall always carry in memory the picture of his manly face and superb form. I was immensely pleased with his growth in maturity, with that world view-point which he had already won, and with the solid purpose of his mind.

Brodrick's travelling companion on the *Lusitania*, Richard Rich Freeman, Jr., '09, was going with him to Russia to join in the mining engineering to which he himself was returning *via* London, where he would doubtless have applied himself again to the work of Belgian Relief. With the doomed ship his personal papers, with records of his professional work, went down. His body was rescued and brought home for burial. It is chiefly from such expressions by Dr. Abercrombie and the following message of sympathy from Mr. Hoover that the quality of the man and his work must be inferred:

Please accept from the Executive Committee of the Commission for relief in Belgium our heartfelt sympathy. Early in the year your son unselfishly devoted his time and energies to this work and won the regard of all who became associated with him. Rest assured that many friends are prepared to do everything necessary. Scott Turner, who survived, was with him several hours after the ship sunk and last saw him supported by two oars and with every possibility of being rescued. He was probably the last passenger to leave the ship and was brave and cheerful throughout.

HOOVER, *Chairman*.

From distant Petrograd a few months later came this letter speaking for the impression which Brodrick's personality and labors had produced in Russia; it was written by a professional and business associate, Mr. J. P. B. Webster:

I write you not only on my own behalf, but also at the request of the Russian directors and employees of the Kyshtim, Irtysh, Tanalyk and Russo-Asiatic Companies to express our very deep sympathy with you in the loss of your son.

Mrs. Webster has already written you of the close friendship between your son and our family, which we so much valued; this was in private life, and also in business his great ability, combined with unfailing courtesy and kind actions, caused him to be held in the highest esteem by a very large circle of Russian friends. His important and successful work at Kyshtim did not prevent him giving individual attention and kindly aid to his assistants, as a result of which, the Kyshtim Geological Department, founded by him, is now looked on as the finest practical school in Russia, men therefrom being eagerly sought to fill important geological posts throughout the Empire; every man who passed through this Kyshtim school during the period when your son was in charge was proud to acknowledge the feelings of personal friendship.

I have just returned to Petrograd from an extended visit to Kyshtim, Tanalyk and the surrounding country; everywhere the deepest horror is felt at the dastardly act which cost your son his life, and I was asked to express to you the sincerest sympathies of a very large circle of Russian friends and admirers of your son.

We have lost a true friend and Russia has lost the most brilliant geologist of recent times.

On the first anniversary of the sinking of the *Lusitania*, May 7, 1916, Professor Josiah Royce delivered a memorable address. A portion of it consisted of a letter from a friend describing the course of Brodrick and others, all unnamed, in sailing on the *Lusitania* to fulfil professional engagements. Royce's words on this matter may well stand as the final words about Carlton Brodrick:

> Benjamin Franklin says, "They that can give up essential liberty to obtain a little temporary safety, deserve neither liberty nor safety." My friend, intuitively enlightened by sorrow, said something deeper than the words of Franklin. Our liberties are dear to us and ought to be so. Our young professional men should be trained to be prepared for dangerous undertakings and dutifully to keep their promises when once these are made. Ralph Waldo Emerson said the well-known word about the conditions under which "'Tis man's perdition to be safe." Such conditions are realized when men make professional engagements. Some of the young men who went down on the *Lusitania* were in this position. They met the requirements defined by Franklin's word and by Emerson's line about the safety that is perdition. We can speak of them as vindicating American rights, and reverence them for their part in doing American duties. They are the men whom we want. Since they met death in such a task, we honor their memory not merely as a matter of personal grief, but as an act of reverence and piety. Blessed are they: "Their works do follow them."

HARRY GUSTAV BYNG

Class of 1913

Though the college affiliations of Harry Gustav Byng were with the Class of 1913, the University Catalogue shows him to have been rated in the first of his two years at Harvard, 1910–11, as an unclassified, in the second, 1911–12, as a special, student. These definitions are applied to men who do not enter College by the regular avenues, and are not — at least not yet — candidates for degrees in the regular course. There was every reason for Byng to stand in precisely this relation with Harvard.

He was an Englishman, born in London, July 12, 1889, the third son of Gustav and Ida Byng. His school was Harrow, where he was captain of the eight, and head of his house. His father was the founder of the General Electric

Company in England, and it was to prepare himself for a position in this great organization that he came to America.

A classmate, Oliver Wolcott, wrote of him in the *Harvard Graduates' Magazine* of September, 1915: "When he decided to come to Harvard he had literally not an acquaintance in the United States, but the charm of his personality and the fineness of his character quickly brought him not acquaintances but friends." If he had entered College with a swarm of friends and remained there four years he could hardly have taken a more definite place among his fellows; for besides becoming a member of the Institute of 1770, D. K. E., Stylus, Signet, Hasty Pudding, Iroquois, and Fly Clubs, he played in both of his two years on the "Soccer" football team, of which he was an admirable captain in the second year, and served on the editorial board of the *Advocate*. His contributions, in articles and fiction, to that journal were English and Scottish in background, and revealed a maturity of thought and sureness of touch which seem a more characteristic product of English than of American schooling.

At Harvard his special study was electrical engineering; for a year after leaving College he was employed at the Schenectady works of the General Electric Company. Thus prepared for the position awaiting him at home he returned to England, and was in the engineering department of the General Electric Company there when the war broke out.

He enlisted at once as a private in a regiment made up of university men, the 28th City of London, known as the "Artists' Rifles," and went to the front in October, 1914, serving as a scout. In the following March he wrote to

Professor Copeland that he was going to take a commission: "Life is much more simple and pleasant as a private amongst friends; but they need officers who have had a certain amount of experience, so there is no help for it." In the same letter he wrote: "At first you worry about the landing places of the shells, but there are so many different noises that, not being able to keep track of them all, it is simpler to ignore them. 'Yer never 'ears the bullet wot cops yer' is the Tommies' philosophy — and is the best one."

In March, 1915, he was gazetted 2d lieutenant in the King's Own Scottish Borderers, known as the Border Regiment. Later in this month, during a four days' leave, he was married in London, March 22, to Miss Evelyn Curtis, of Boston, a daughter of Allen Curtis, of the Harvard Class of 1884.

Returning immediately to the front he took up with zest the officer's life, of which less than two months remained to him. His letters and diary show him playing, and enjoying soccer, taking a hearty pleasure in meeting friends from the "Artists," keenly interested in the men of his command. An undercurrent of serious thinking expresses itself from time to time. "The Parson was fifteen minutes late" — he wrote one day about Church Parade — "and altogether the service was a failure. Personally I don't care a bit now — unless the man is really good; I am thinking my own thoughts all the time." A little later he wrote, "To early Communion with Lindsay" — and a few days later still, April 2, "Good Friday and I forgot it — ashamed of myself." Not all the scenes of horror go unnoted: "There are dead bodies hanging on the barbed wire — one Ghurka strangling a German. Then there is a little grave bearing the epitaph, 'Some one's leg.'" Now and then one surprises him in a furtive act of kindness: "This morning I came across two artillery limbers all shattered and in one grave next to them three men were buried. It was pathetic. The names were neatly printed on the cross, with their regimental numbers, etc. I took two pictures of it, and if it is good, we will have enlargements made and sent to the men's wives or mothers. I am sure it would mean a lot to them."

Here are a few longer passages from Byng's letters in the final weeks of his life:

We relieved the Grenadier Guards. The men are a fine lot, but now that the original officers are gone, I was not much impressed by their substitutes, and the result is of course that the men get stale. It is a point of etiquette in the service to hand over your trenches clean to your relief. Well this was not really bad, but not nearly so clean as our C. O. insists ours must be. Johnson and I are sharing quite a palatial dugout which we took over from two Lords. It is always rather confusing the first night, but we got fixed up finally, and I got some sleep from one to five. This morning we cleaned up, as far as possible, but it is not very possible, as there are flooded parts everywhere and about five inches of sticky wet clay. We arranged cook houses, refuse pits, loop holes, etc., and were not called down by the C. O. — that is his highest form of praise. Life is not slack in the trenches.

It is now 10.45 and at 12.30 we march off to be inspected by French. We have had a parade from nine to ten this morning to see that the men are ready. There are one hundred and one little things you have to inspect — shaving, haircut, boots cleaned, buttons all there, rifles and bayonets, packs neat and waterproof sheets properly folded, equipments properly adjusted, belts tight, puttees on properly, etc. Personally I hate these inspections, and having been a Tommy myself, I know how much they irritate the men, but it is all part of the discipline. The whole aim and object of this hard and fast discipline is to make obedience an instinctive habit with the men, so that in a crisis they do what they are told. It is the same kind of idea when Harvard trains three months for a football match that is over in an hour — the only difference is that our test may come at any moment and so there can be no second allowed for breaking training. I must confess I don't like the life a great deal, and after the war, I shall get out of the regular Army, as soon as I can.

We are still very unsettled — yesterday morning we were told that we should probably stay in for a long time — eighteen days, and then suddenly we were warned to be ready to hand over our trenches tomorrow (that is today). The officer of the relieving regiment came up this morning, as usual, to look round, and this afternoon we are told that the relief is cancelled, so we don't know where we are at all. It gets a little trying after a week as you feel the lack of sleep. Personally, though, I stand it pretty well — the night shift at Schenectady taught me to sleep during the day. I bought my platoon flannel strips for use against the gases, but so far we have not been troubled — I am not very much scared of them. But the Germans are dirty fighters in every way. The chief unpleasantness of these trenches is the unburied dead all around in between the lines — directly we try to bury them, our parties get fired on, so they have to be left. You get used to it, just as you do to everything else — a dead body really means nothing at all, it simply shows, that all that is worth anything of the person has gone somewhere else. From a purely sanitary point of view they are a danger, though. One of our patrols yesterday brought in a pocket book taken from a dead German — he was born in 1897 — pretty young to get killed. We have rumors here that we did very well north of Ypres last night — exploded their own gas and shelled them heavily. How true it is, I don't know.

We were relieved last night about eleven — Lord, I was pleased! I was in a detached post, right out from our lines. I just had my platoon, about fifty men, two machine-guns, and six bomb-throwers. In a way I was pleased to go, as they send the best platoon and the best officer from each company, and everybody took it as a matter of course that I should take my number nine — they really are quite a splendid lot. You have to patrol rather a lot — it is nervous work, but really fairly safe. You crawl along about ten yards and then you flop and stay still and listen. The chief trouble up there was avoiding the dead bodies. I was really pleased with the men — the usual routine is two hours on sentry and four off. I had to have two hours on and two hours off, but they never complained, and yet in billets they grouse all day long.

I had quite a compliment paid me yesterday: the Brigadier wanted a very important patrol done, and as it was on our part of the line, it was up to the Border Regiment to do it. Well, of course they never send Senior Officers on them, and I was told privately (by Bobby) that when the Brigadier asked for the best man for the job, I was chosen at once, thanks to my training as a scout. We had to find out the kind of obstacle to an advance that a ditch would be which ran about forty yards in front of one of our advance posts. The Germans are only about eighty yards away, so it needs care — the grass is getting long now and really it is not half so dangerous as it sounds. In fact, unless they see you — and it is up to you to take care that they don't — everything being aimed at the tops of the parapets is miles above you. Of course you crawl all the time. I am getting quite used to patrols now. Personally, I got too far to the left, but as a patrol we got at the conformation required and the C. O. was quite pleased about it, and sent me and Goodman up to the Brigadier himself. I was just about to start on the trip last night after finishing your letter. I only got in at four this morning, but I am going to have a long sleep tonight.

On May 12 Byng wrote in similar vein of his assignment to patrol duty: "It is a darn dangerous job, but it is vitally necessary for the attack, and it is a great compliment (a doubtful one, perhaps) to be picked out for it." He was leading his men, as acting captain, in an attack at Festubert on May 16 when he received the wounds of which he died in a field hospital two days later. He "fell on the enemy's trenches," his commanding officer wrote, "where he lay all day, since the stretcher-bearers could not reach him until nightfall." It is also told by a friend that he would not let his men carry him to the rear, lest they themselves should be needlessly exposed in the process; thus he lay uncomplaining from three in the morning till eight at night, when it was possible to move him in safety to the hospital.

He is buried at Béthune in Picardie.

HENRY WESTON FARNSWORTH

CLASS OF 1912

HENRY FARNSWORTH was the first of the Harvard men fallen in the war whose name is enshrined in a permanent memorial touching the daily lives of students at Harvard. The Farnsworth Room in the Widener Library Building, a room full of books to be read merely for pleasure, and in a comforting quiet, symbolizes with special aptness the sanctuary which this young man, through the brief span of a life crowded with more than the commonly allotted share of vivid experience, found in the best reading, pictures, and music.

He was born in Dedham, Massachusetts, August 7, 1890, the son of William Farnsworth of the Harvard Class of 1877, and Lucy Holman (Burgess) Farnsworth. When he was twelve he went to Groton School, whence he proceeded to Harvard College, as a member of the Class of 1912. An anecdote related in the "Foreword" to a privately printed volume of his letters suggests the difficulties he was always to encounter in following the trodden paths of convention:

> When eleven he went to a day-school in Boston. It was his first contact with the outside world. One day, after he had been to school for a few weeks, he came home three hours late, and said, "Mother, if you were a man, would you want to experience life? I felt that way this afternoon, and I have had a soda in every soda-water fountain in Boston."

This early desire to experience life was destined to carry him far afield. His first summer vacation gave him a taste of camping in the West, an initiation into the beauty of "letting nature have its way." Early in his sophomore year, dissatisfied with the mode of life into which he had fallen at college, he resolved to follow his own bent, to test his own resources, and, without informing his family of his plans, shipped as a deck-hand on a cattle-ship sailing for England. His hopes of maintaining himself by his pen proved delusive, and, in response to an advertisement of work to be had at a sheep station in Australia, he sailed steerage in a small steamer, bound for Melbourne. "Lord, I wish I was coming into the tropics again for the first time," he wrote afterwards. "I came through the Suez Canal, and struck the East all in a heap. Nineteen years of age, and a head full of all kinds of rot at that." The magic of Eastern names — especially Rangoon, Singapore, Parang — bewitched him. "What romance I had in those days, and how quick I lost it too, — that fool kind, I mean, like calf love."

Romance met with rough handling when Farnsworth first stepped ashore in Australia. This was at Fremantle, where his ship stopped on its way to Melbourne. Returning to the vessel after dark, and passing through a rough part of the town, he was set upon, knocked senseless, and robbed of everything, even his shoes. Fortunately he was able to reach the ship before its sailing, but, utterly stranded in Melbourne, without money even to travel on to the sheep station he had come so far to find, he was obliged to pocket his pride and cause a cable to be sent to his father, asking for a little money. "All the rest of his life," says the "Foreword" to his "Letters," "he never forgot that the first act of his struggle for independence was a cry for help, when he had travelled to the other side of the world to try to help himself."

The help that came from home enabled him to spend seven months in Australia as a sheep-herder, exercising his skill in horsemanship, and at the same time doing the hard, solitary thinking which brought him home again in time for the next year of study at college. With him this took the form of a wide range of reading in many literatures, paralleled by the eager hearing of all the good music within reach. Through attending the Harvard Engineering Camp in the summer of 1911, he made up enough of his interrupted studies to graduate with his class in 1912. That summer he passed in Europe, especially Russia, and, joining his family in Paris, returned to enter the Graduate School of Business Administration in the autumn. Then the Balkan War broke out, and Farnsworth hastened to the scene of it.

The record of his experiences in that upheaval of the Near East is preserved in a volume, "The Log of a Would-be War Correspondent" which he published a year later. The news of "trouble in Balkans," Farnsworth wrote, "seemed to be received with calm interest by the public; but in me it started a veritable fire." His narrative of the results showed him chiefly occupied with frantic but unavailing endeavors to have himself attached to the Turkish Army as an accredited correspondent. Failing in this, he mounted himself on a little stallion which he named John Henry Newman ("John Henry" for short), set forth loudly whistling the Eroica Symphony in the zest of his private adventure towards the front, there ran imminent risks of cholera and shell fire, saw much of ghastly and entertaining realities, and wrote about them afterwards with a liveliness of apprehension and description worthy of something more than a "would-be correspondent."

Returning to America he took up his studies in the Harvard Business School through the spring of 1913, and in the autumn of that year, having determined to make writing his occupation, seized an opportunity to become an actual war correspondent, in Mexico, for the Providence *Journal*. His letters were printed on the editorial page of that newspaper, and on his return to the United States he served, in the winter of 1913–14, on its staff of reporters. Back again to Mexico he went when American troops were landed at Vera Cruz, and he was in Mexico City when the European War broke out. He came home immediately, to receive his heart's desire when his family, unimportuned, consented to his setting forth to Europe. There he meant to look on and write about what he saw. Before the end of

October he was in Paris, and ready to join an independent fighting corps in case of its acceptance by the British Government. This was not accorded, and after a visit to Spain and a lonely month in the Island of Mallorca, Farnsworth found himself back in Paris, where the cause of Francc took such hold upon him that on January 1, 1915, with the cabled consent of his family, he enlisted in the Foreign Legion for the duration of the war.

His printed letters show what manner of man he was, what manner of life he led in the Legion, more clearly than could anything else. Let the following passages tell their story:

PARIS, *January 5, 1915.*

I formally and definitely joined the *Légion Étrangère* this morning, and tomorrow morning I go into barracks here in Paris, and as soon as the company is ready, on to the front. The joining was to me very solemn. After being stripped and examined as carefully as a horse, and given a certificate of "aptitude" I went to another place and was sworn in. A little old man with two medals and a glistening eye looked over my papers and then in a strong voice asked if I was prepared to become a soldier of France and, if asked to, lay down my life for her cause. Then I signed, and was told to report the next morning and be prepared to start training at once.

I went out and walked down the Boulevard des Invalides, with Napoleon's tomb behind me. It was warm and foggy, and the golden-winged horses on the Pont Alexandre III seemed to be stirring through the mist. Lately I have come to love Paris beyond all cities, and now I think in a dim way I can understand how the French love it.

PARIS, *January 9, 1915.*

In the first place, there is no tough element at all. Many of the men are educated, and the very lowest is of the high-class workman type. In my room, for instance, there are "Le Petit

Père Uhlin," an old Alsatian, who has already served fourteen years in the Legion in China and Morocco; the Corporal Lebrun, a Socialist well known in his own district; Engler, a Swiss cotton broker from Havre; Donald Campbell, a newspaper man and short-story writer, who will not serve in the English army because his family left England in 1745, with the exception of his father, who was Captain in the Royal Irish Fusiliers; Sukuna, a Fijian student at Oxford, black as ink; Hath, a Dane, over six feet, whom Campbell aptly calls "The Blonde Beast" (*vide* "Zarathustra"); Von somebody, another Dane, very small and young; Bastados, a Swiss carpenter, born and bred in the Alps, who sings — when given half a litre of canteen wine — far better than most comic opera stars, and who at times does the *Ranz des Vaches* so that even Petit Père Uhlin claps; the brigadier Mussorgsky, cousin descendant of the composer, a little Russian; two or three Polish Jews, nondescript Belgians, Greeks, Roumanians, etc. I already have enough to write a long (ten thousand word) article, and at the end of the campaign can write a book truly interesting.

PARIS, *January 17, 1915.*

The other day I bought a pair of boots and was at the *caisse* paying for them, when the manager of the shop dashed up and said he would not take any payment from "*un des petits Légionnaires.*" I explained to him that I had plenty of money, but that if he would give me a reduction, I would see that the difference went where it would be really appreciated. He gave me ten francs off, and I gave five to Le Petit Père Uhlin and five to de Hath, a Dane and a gentleman, explaining of course how I got the money. Uhlin sent a money order to his wife in Alsace, and de Hath bought a pair of gloves. I mention this episode because it is a good example of the way things go in our company. Although Uhlin has spent hours showing me how to take down the rifle, to grease boots, fence with the bayonet, polish my belt, etc., I have never dared offer him any money, although I knew he had not a cent except the five centimes per day that is the regulation pay.

About March 7, 1915.
(*After moving toward the front.*)

Then came the magic of the nights. At sundown we began to do sentry, hour on and hour off till daylight. We were about fifty metres from the German trenches and not allowed to shoot (why, I don't know). As the night grows, and you stand crouching and watching for any sign of life ahead of you, the very air seems to come to life. All is still, nobody talks above a whisper, and all lights are out. From trenches, all along the maze of line, shots crack out and stray impersonal bullets whiz by on unknown errands. A huge rocket candle shoots up and hangs for a moment above the earth, lighting up a section of the country, big guns boom out, and shells like witches riding to a feast whiz by. Sometimes, with a whistle and bang, a half-dozen "75's" swoop over like a covey of devil's quail, and we stand crouching and watching for any sign of human life. It never came. Just the impersonal bang and whistle.

May 30, 1915.

Of the last six days in the lines, *rien à signaler*, except two patrols, which lacked nothing but the Germans to make them successful. Between the lines is a broad fertile field of beet sugar and clover. It is grown high enough to hide a man crawling on his stomach, and in spots, even on all fours. It is here that the patrols take place. The first was an attempted ambuscade. Fifteen of us, with an adjutant, a sergeant, and two corporals, went out and hid in a spot where Germans had been seen twice before. None appeared. The next night seven of us were detailed to carry French papers, telling of Italy's declaration of war, into the German lines. We crawled from 9 o'clock till 11.30, and succeeded in sticking papers on their barbed wire. They have since then steadily ignored them, much to our disgust.

There is a certain fascination in all this, dull though it may seem. The patrol is selected in the afternoon. At sunset we meet to make the plans and tell each man his duty; then at dark our pockets are filled with cartridges, a drawn bayonet in the belt, and our magazines loaded to the brim. We go along the *boyau* to the *petit poste* from which it is decided to leave. All along the line the sentinels wish us good luck and a safe return. In the *petit poste* we clamp on the bayonets, blow noses, clear throats, and prepare for three hours of utter silence. At a word from the chief we form line in the prearranged order. The sentries wish us luck for the last time, and the chief jumps up on the edge of the trenches and begins to work his way quickly through the barbed wire. Once outside he disappears in the beet weeds and one after another we follow.

Then begins the crawl to the appointed spot. We go slowly, with frequent halts. Every sound must be analyzed. On the occasion of the would-be ambush, I admit I went to sleep after a while in the warm fresh clover where we lay. It was the adjutant himself who woke me up with a slight hiss; but as he chose me again next night, he does not seem to have thought it a serious matter.

Then, too, once home we do not mount guard all the rest of the night, and are allowed to sleep in the morning; also there are small, but pleasing, discussions of the affair, and above all the hope of some night suddenly leaping out of the darkness hand to hand with the Germans.

August 13, 1915.

We will probably go to the trenches shortly. If so, so much the better; but if we are liberated, I think I shall dash home by the first boat and stay there a month or six weeks and get my "Campaign with the Legion" written and then try to get back again in the Aviation or Ambulance, or anything that Papa approves. This seems too ideally happy ever to come true — worse than that, I dreamt the whole thing last night, and my dreams never come true.

September 16, 1915.

I was in the ranks . . . this morning, when, a division being drawn up, M. Poincaré and M. Millerand and Général de Castelnau, and a lot of others, presented the regiment with a flag decorated with the *grande Croix de Guerre* . . . . The President's speech was good, and very short, and addressed — it is characteristic of the French attitude towards the Legion — to the Zouaves and *tirailleurs*, the fourth regiment of the latter having received a flag as well. He spoke of the Marne, where the Division broke the Prussian guard, and ended up with a ringing praise for the action north of Arras. It was also characteristic that the Legion received its flag before the others, and that our Colonel gave the commands.

I shall write again in three or four days. Now I must go and bathe in a mountain stream. Thirty-five kilometers on top of the review and the defile make it necessary.

Less than a fortnight later Farnsworth was killed in the Battle of Champagne. His friend, the Fijian prince, who had been a student at Oxford, thus wrote of Farnsworth's last fight, and of his own debt of life to his comrade:

HOSPITAL COMPLIMENTAIRE, 17 PRÉ AUX CLERCS,
LYON (BRETTAUX), FRANCE,
October 2, 1915.

DEAR MR. FARNSWORTH:

At the request of your son, I am to say with real pain that he was severely wounded on the afternoon of the 28th of September last, on the fourth day of the battle of Champagne, a little in front of the German wire entanglements of the second line before the Fortin de Navarin. A large number of machine guns were on the right flank, and in front, where they were concentrating their fire on the leading files of the attacking party, and no stretcher-bearer could possibly reach the spot where he was lying. Toward dusk, the column was still being held up. I left for the rear about this time, but all I could do, I regret to say, was to ask medical people to go up if possible. As one who has seen a great deal of him here, I would venture to mention how much his coolness under fire has on occasions helped to steady the section, and how his indifference to danger prompted him at all times to volunteer for the most dangerous posts. Under a withering rifle and machine gun fire, he denied my first word and dug a hole for me, to which act I probably owe my life. Up to the present, no fresh information of him has come my way, but I shall always be glad to furnish any previous news. May I here express my profound and sincere sympathies.

Very truly yours,

J. L. V. SUKUNA.

And Victor Chapman, not of Groton but of St. Paul's School, wrote thus of his college contemporary and fellow *Légionnaire:*

CAMP D'AVORD, *November 2, 1915.*

TO GROTON SCHOOL, GROTON, MASSACHUSETTS:

I suppose you have heard by now that Henry Farnsworth was killed in the last days of September. A brave fellow he was and a gallant one. The two or three times I met him at college he made little impression. But of the months I knew him in the Legion, I respected him and enjoyed his companionship more and more. When everything was going badly — we were disreputably officered in the *3me de marche*—and every man was finding fault, grumbling, making all the possible steps to get out of the Legion into French regiments, he was always optimistic, serene, and an immense moral force in his company. "Leave the Legion? Never!" When we were transferred to the *2me de marche* and the true Legion, then he was exultant. Many of the *3me* felt insulted to be put with these "desperate characters"; but he only told them since they had come to fight, they should be the more happy to be put with the most fearless, perhaps the most famous regiment in France, since the 9th of May and 16th of June. I know he could have wished for nothing more glorious than to die as he did when the *1ère Étrangère* again covered itself with honor on the 29th. The *Tirailleurs Algériens* flinched on the right, but his Battalion went on and was demolished.

VICTOR CHAPMAN.

CHARLES ROBERT CROSS, Jr.

Class of 1903

Charles Robert Cross, Jr., was a veritable son of New England. Through his father, Charles Robert Cross, Thayer Professor of Physics in the Massachusetts Institute of Technology, he traced descent from Robert Cross, who settled in Ipswich, Massachusetts, about 1635, and became a soldier in the Pequot War; through his mother, Mariana (Pike) Cross, from Robert Pike, who came to Salisbury, also in 1635, and is remembered, as Professor Cross has said in an unpublished account of his son from which most of this memoir is directly and indirectly drawn, "for his just treatment of the Quakers and his denunciation of the Witchcraft delusion."

Robert, or "Bob," Cross, as his friends habitually called him, was born in Roxbury, Boston, June 17, 1881. Prepared for college at Noble and Greenough's School in Boston, he passed his entrance examinations to Harvard in 1898, with Greek, and without a condition. "Indeed," his father adds, "he never made a failure in school, college, or professional school."

As eighteen was believed a better age than seventeen for him to enter Harvard, he passed the academic year of 1898–99 as a student at the Massachusetts Institute of Technology, applying himself with good results to science and languages, with which he was credited in his college course. This preliminary work and faithful, though not the hardest, study in college qualified him for his degree in 1902, but he remained with his class until its graduation in 1903, having aimed rather at general cultivation than at mastery in any single field intensively worked. A true fondness for music kept him diligently practising at the piano through college and beyond.

Already he had become an "outdoors man." Dissuaded from the more violent athletics by the family physician, Cross spent much of his time during his undergraduate years at the Oakley Country Club, developing a fine physique through open-air exercises. As a boy he had greatly enjoyed climbing in the White Mountains. His love of mountain scenery and nature in its solitudes was nourished during his college course by the use to which he put his summer vacations. At the end of his freshman year he visited the Canadian Rockies and had his first experience of snow-climbing with guides. In each of the next three summers he travelled in Europe, and in 1901 and 1902 made some notable ascents in the Alps.

From 1903 to 1906, when he took the degree of LL.B., he was a student working hard and maintaining an excellent position in the Harvard Law School. In 1907 he was admitted to the Massachusetts Bar. Before he entered upon the practice of his profession he spent another year at the Institute of Technology, in the expectation of devoting himself especially to patent law. Finding that other branches of the profession really interested him more, he abandoned this intention and in the autumn of 1907 entered the law office of Boyden, Palfrey, Bradlee & Twombly, in Boston. Here he remained until 1913, when he withdrew, meaning to open an office of his own or to enter business. But a long summer expedition, for the double purpose of exploration and of restoring himself to normal health after an extended period of professional labor, was to come first. He had then been out of college ten years, and his own account of himself, written for the Decennial Report of his class, will show, better than any paraphrase of his words, what the years had brought to him — and he to them:

As I glance back at the time that has passed since I became a graduate, it seems that my life has been governed by two gods: the spirit of modern civilization that gathers its slaves together in cities, and goads them on to toil in the crowded rounds of business, medicine, or law, striving for money and fame among men; and the red spirit of the wilderness and the wild, that leads its followers, regardless of the consequences, in search of the still places of the earth and regions where nature yet holds undisputed reign.

The first of these two masters carried me through the Harvard Law School, from which I graduated in 1906, through two summers and a winter in Technology, and finally, into an office in the city of Boston, in which office I still am and where for the last four or five years I have worked in the practice of law. The second of my masters has led me not only through the woods and mountains and upon the streams of New England, but also on journeys to regions remote and unfrequented. During the first four years after leaving the Law School I hunted for many months in the Northwest; I saw a summer pass and a fall while I travelled the woods and mountains of the upper Stikine and the headwaters of the Mackenzie in search of bear and moose and sheep; a spring came and a summer went as I wandered among the snowy cloud-shrouded peaks of the Alaska peninsula, trailing the great brown bear in his haunts by the Behring Sea; and again as I followed the bear and the white sheep of the North over the ragged mountains of the Kenai, the fall days grew short and the winter's snows drove down. And in the last three years, even since I perforce have become closely bound to the city and a lawyer's work therein, still my red god has led me each fall for a few weeks to the marshes and barrens of Newfoundland, where the caribou yet move ghost-like among the woods and through the fogs driving low across the opens, and where, as in Saltatha's country of the musk ox, "the lakes are sometimes misty and sometimes blue and the loons cry often."

The summer expedition of 1913 took Robert Cross, with Mr. Edward Preble of the United States Biological Survey, into the scantily explored region of Lake Babine in British Columbia, east of the Skeena River. The presence and species of the mountain sheep of this region were the special objects of his study. From this expedition he returned to Boston late in the autumn of 1913, and in the spring of 1914 was still weighing the merits of possible permanent employments in business and the law when the opportunity came to join his friend S. Prescott Fay (Harvard, '07) in exploring the region of British Columbia between the Yellow

Head Pass and Peace River, in which Mr. Fay had already travelled. It was the last large area of British Columbia from which it was to be hoped that much fresh scientific information could be brought. An account of the successes, hardships, and pleasures encountered by the two explorers, accompanied by Mr. Fred Brewster of Jasper, Alberta, with two helpers and twenty head of horses, was contributed by Mr. Fay to *Appalachia* for June, 1915. From this and other far northern expeditions Cross brought home noble trophies of the hunt in the form of heads and skins, some of which are to be seen in the "Aesculapian Room" of the Harvard Club of Boston, where they have been placed by the Harvard Travellers Club, of which Cross was first a member and then a fellow. Reports of his several explorations in Alberta, British Columbia, and Alaska were duly made to the United States Biological Survey, and of those in Newfoundland to the Agent of the Newfoundland Railway.

Emerging from the wilds at a station of the Hudson's Bay Company, in October, 1914, Cross and his companions first heard of the war in Europe. "It must be a fierce state of affairs," he immediately wrote home. Late in November the party arrived at Jasper, whence it had set forth in June, and before the end of the year Cross was back in Boston. His mind was promptly made up to go to Europe and do what he could in the cause of the Allies. The thought of seeking a commission in the Canadian Army was rejected because he felt so strongly that the time must, and should, come when his own country would join the belligerents, and that his strength should be kept for that day. He had been a member of Battery A of the Massachusetts Militia from 1905 to 1911, and, with all his skill in marksmanship and in outdoor pursuits, ashore and afloat, must have been conscious of a rare capacity for the physical struggle of war. For the present, however, the best opportunity for usefulness seemed to lie in some form of relief service, and without knowing just what that form should be — since all this work was less definitely organized then than later — he sailed for Havre on January 20, 1915.

A severe attack of bronchitis in Paris delayed his entrance upon active, though temporary, employment as a driver for the American Ambulance at Dunkirk. Having entered this service with the understanding that he could leave it at will because he was meeting all his own expenses, he soon joined the American Distributing Service, an agency organized and maintained from the very beginning of the war by the wife of Robert Woods Bliss, of the Harvard Class of 1900, counsellor of the American Embassy at Paris. Its special mission was the collection and delivery of supplies to hospitals, of which, with a small but devoted staff, it was then serving more than seven hundred. The appeal which this service made to Cross was, as he wrote home, that "it is real work that counts," and, moreover, that "they are planning to move their work into Poland and perhaps Serbia."

The move to Serbia came earlier than could have been expected. Indeed he had hardly begun his work with the American Distributing Service in Paris when Dr. Richard P. Strong, Professor of Tropical Medicine in the Harvard Medical School, who had come to Paris with the Harvard Surgical Unit for a term of service at the American Ambulance Hospital in Paris, became director of the American

Red Cross Sanitary Commission to Serbia, financed by the Red Cross and the Rockefeller Foundation, and asked Cross to join him, as executive assistant, in the great fight against typhus. Here was work for a man who had conducted expeditions of his own through difficult countries. His hands were at once filled with manifold details. "I have been on the dead jump," he wrote to America, "ever since Dr. Strong told me he wanted me to come with him if I cared to go. I have been acting the part of 'courier' for him, getting the necessary papers to get out of France and making arrangements for the journey. It has seemed best to get an entire camp outfit, as we shall be in Nish a week before the outfit arrives *via* Salonica, for we go *via* Berne, Vienna, Budapest, Sofia, etc., and hotels may not be safe. . . . I felt there was a lot of work to be done and not too many who wanted to do it. I felt also that the work undertaken by Strong and Shattuck and the rest was a great one. . . . As for the risk, for there is undoubtedly a risk, it seemed to me that if Strong and Shattuck could take it I could."

A letter from Nish, the ancient Roman city of Nissa, described the places through which he passed with Dr. Strong on his way to Serbia, the familiar view of the Alps from Berne, the tension of feeling and the phenomenon of bread-tickets in Vienna, the liveliness and beauty of Budapest, the oriental aspect of Bucharest, the antiquity and strangeness of Nish itself. From Skoplje, where Dr. Strong began his work, Cross made trips with him to "typhus villages," to Belgrade, and other places. The transportation of sorely needed supplies was a task of the first importance. When Cross felt that he had done all that a layman might to prepare the way for the physicians' work of sanitation, he was making ready, late in May, to return to Paris. Just at this time Dr. Strong found that conditions in Montenegro were such that a dangerous outbreak of typhus could be prevented only by decisive measures. Dr. F. B. Grinnell (Harvard, '09), of Dr. Strong's staff, was accordingly detailed to Montenegro. None of the other medical men could be spared. "So Grinnell was up against it," Cross wrote on May 27 in a letter from Skoplje, "both for a companion and a person to help manage the game. He then asked me whether I would be willing to lend him a hand, and of course I said yes. When the other seventy-five docs from the States get here one or two will come over to assist, and probably there will be no more need for me."

The pressure of the immediate need was revealed by Cross's saying in the letter just quoted, "This morning we started sixty bullock wagons of medical supplies, etc., down on the train to a place that sounds like Mitravika [Mitrovitza?], and we follow tomorrow morning and will proceed day after tomorrow, if there are no delays, to Montenegro."

Professor Cross has written, in the sketch of his son:

No letters were received from Montenegro, several having been lost in the mails. . . . Dr. George Shattuck told me that on the arrival of Dr. Grinnell and Robert at Pech in Montenegro, which they were to make their headquarters, the Bishop of Pech invited them to establish themselves within the monastery walls, since, as he told them, the Albanians would attack and kill them if they slept outside. Naturally they accepted the invitation which indeed must have been welcome on other grounds. Shortly after, the Bishop invited them to dine with him and so enjoyable did the occasion prove that he further asked them to do the same habitually while they were there, which they did. I further judge that the Bishop was pleased with them personally as among the very few films which came home with Robert's effects there were several of the Bishop who had evidently "stood for his picture" arrayed in his robes of office.

Of all the Serbian experience Cross's father has written besides:

It has been said of him by those associated in the work there that he was always cheerful, and when the supplies, of whose transportation he had charge, seemed unreasonably slow in coming was never disheartened but always confident that they would arrive in due time, as they in fact did, and this attitude was a very encouraging one to his comrades; also that he was a "tremendous" worker at all times, doing his utmost to facilitate matters.

He lamented in one of his letters his inability to speak Serbian, but it illustrates his desire to "facilitate matters" that among his belongings there was afterwards found a Serbian phrase-book, from which he had doubtless been trying to win some use of the language.

Cross paid his first visit to Greece on his way back to Paris, where again he plunged into the labors of the American Distributing Service, dividing his long days between work in the warehouse and on the road. Devoted as he was to this Service and to his companions in it, the distress of seeing so much suffering which he could not help and the desire for more active employment in the open had begun to turn his thoughts strongly to aviation. *Dis aliter visum.*

The story of the accident which cut short his life is told in his father's narrative. His companion at the time, Russell H. Greeley (Harvard '01), director of the American Distributing Service, completely recovered from his serious injury, and during his convalescence received the Cross of the Legion of Honor with the thanks of the French Government for the noble humanitarian work which he and many of his countrymen had done since the beginning of the war. Thus writes Professor Cross:

On October 4, 1915, with Russell Greeley he left St. Brieuc, where they had spent the previous night, with a light Ford automobile to finish an inspection tour of the hospitals in that region. Late in the afternoon, as they were entering the little village of Ploubalay, a peasant woman appeared driving a few cows one of which became frightened at the sound of the motor. The sheep-dog in chasing the cow ran directly in front of the auto which was driven by Robert. Every effort on his part to steer the auto so that the dog might pass between the wheels failed and it went under a front wheel. The machine swerved toward the left, "the right front wheel struck a pile of broken stones by the left side of the road while the left fore wheel went into the roadside ditch and struck its side. . . . The car was thrown into the air and it turned completely over backwards falling with the wheels in the air and turned in the opposite direction from that in which it had been running."

Greeley was thrown free from the car, but Robert was pinned down. Both were seriously injured, the former with a broken pelvis, the latter with an injury to the spine such that he was paralyzed from the armpits down. It appeared later that the fourth, fifth, and sixth vertebrae were absolutely crushed. Robert fully appreciated the magnitude of his injury at the time and told Greeley upon their being rescued that he knew his neck was broken but that he might live for some time.

At Greeley's request the two victims of this disaster were borne to the French Military Hospital No. 64 at Dinard, a few kilometers distant. Here they were both known in person through their work in the American Distributing Service; indeed the very supplies which they had delivered were drawn upon for their comfort. The action of the *médecin chef* in receiving civilians into a military hospital was at once confirmed by his superiors, and directions were issued that they should be officially treated as "officers wounded in service." Mrs. Bliss and other members of the Service made all haste to Dinard. When they entered the hospital room where the two men lay, Cross, though knowing well the seriousness of his injury, exclaimed, "Well, we're all right — no one is going to die in this room." Dr. Pierre Duval, a Paris diagnostician and surgeon of the highest skill, was immediately called in. An X-ray examination showed that a dangerous operation offered the only hope of life. To this, with a full knowledge of all the possibilities involved, Cross decided to submit, asking only that the news of the accident should not be cabled to his father until after the operation. In its direct results it proved successful. For two days his condition steadily improved. Then there was a sudden loss of strength, and on Friday evening, October 8, 1915, in spite of the best care which skill and devotion could supply, he died. The courage of his bearing through all the ordeal of these final days, his serenity, humor, consideration for others, impressed profoundly both the friends and the strangers amongst whom Robert Cross came to his untimely end. It chanced to be the birthday of one of these, who turned to another, and said: "No birthday gift could be more splendid than to have brought into one's life so wonderful an example of courage and manhood."

A funeral service, attended by distinguished representatives of the French Government, and of several hospitals and other agencies of mercy, was held in the American Episcopal Church in Paris on October 22. Burial was made later at Newburyport, the home of the family for many generations. No monument or tribute can so fitly commemorate him as a dominating, glacier-clad peak in an unbroken wilderness, a region of lakes in the Canadian Rockies, about seventy-five miles north of the nearest point on the Grand Trunk Pacific Railway. To this mountain the Geographic Board of Canada has given the name of Mount Cross.

ARCHIBALD HAMILTON RAMSAY

CLASS OF 1907

BORN in Montreal, May 31, 1884, Archibald Hamilton Ramsay was a son of the late Robert Anstruther Ramsay, Q.C., of Montreal, and Catherine Hamilton (Duff) Ramsay. He was a member of Harvard College only through the freshman year of the Class of 1907. His preparation for college was made at Highbury House, England, and for the last two years of schooling at the Newton High School. At this time, his family having left Montreal about 1900, and his parents having died, he was living with his brothers and sister at Wellesley Hills, near Boston. A classmate at Newton and at Harvard, where he was also a roommate, writes of his unusually bright mind, especially for mathematics and the classical languages, and also of a happy-go-lucky, somewhat irresponsible quality which kept him from much effort in his college courses. It was the less needed because from the first he purposed spending merely a year at Harvard in preparation for the study of science at the English Cambridge. This plan he carried out, and was a member of Pembroke College from 1903 to 1907. His Harvard friends and classmates remembered him well as a keen sportsman, interested especially in shooting, attractive in personality, and gifted with more than common abilities. "I can best illustrate his unusual brightness," says the friend already quoted, "by citing the fact that when we all gathered in Cambridge for Entrance Examinations, he was pretty near the first man to finish his paper in each subject and leave the examination, taking perhaps only half the full time allowed, and yet obtaining excellent marks."

After leaving Pembroke College Ramsay travelled for a year in Europe, and then for a year (1908–09) was secretary to an official writer. From 1909 till the outbreak of the war he lived in Paris, employed for the first two years by the Westinghouse Company in a capacity partly technical, partly commercial, and from 1911 till August, 1914, as an exchange specialist in an Anglo-French bank dealing with South America. During these years in Paris Ramsay became a well-known figure in business, social, and athletic circles. His athletic interest at this time was concerned chiefly with boxing. A sympathetic writer in the English periodical, *Boxing*, has described Ramsay's faithful attendance on "big fight nights," his own ambition to win the French amateur championship in the ring, and the part he bore in the formation of a club designed to stand in Paris for what the National Sporting Club represented in London.

Thirty and unmarried when the war broke out, he was obviously of the type to which the Foreign Legion would appeal; and in this command he enlisted as a private, August 12, 1914. His knowledge of languages caused him to be detached for special duty as chauffeur and interpreter with the British and French liaison staff — a service which he performed so well that his requests to be transferred to the fighting forces were refused. Thus he remained with the Legion until the spring of 1915. When it became possible for British-born members of the Legion to be transferred to Kitchener's Army, Ramsay at once availed of this opportunity, in April secured his release, and in June was commissioned second lieutenant in the Oxfordshire and Buckinghamshire Light Infantry. Here again his special aptitudes involved him in special duties, and he was made an instructor in physical culture and bombing. Here again he asked for more dangerous duty, and, foregoing a promotion within reach, was sent to the front. He joined his battalion September 25, and on October 13, 1915, was killed in action while leading a forlorn hope bomb attack on the Hohenzollern Redoubt at Loos. It was for bombing that he volunteered, when it was known that a grenade officer's life at the front was estimated at a duration of seven days. In the party of twenty-five of which he was the leader on the day of his death, only five returned. Ramsay was one of the first to fall. His body was not recovered. A tablet in the British Embassy Church at Paris commemorates him.

GEORGE STETSON TAYLOR

CLASS OF 1908

GEORGE STETSON TAYLOR was one of the Americans who, in the earliest days of the war, felt that he must take his part in it, at least in helping to relieve the sufferings of the combatants. The "enthusiasm and energy" which the secretary of his class has noted as highly characteristic of him in college were illustrated in the second month of the war, when he dropped the business in which he had established himself, sailed for England, and sought to make himself useful.

He was born in Orange, New Jersey, May 22, 1886. His parents were Thomas Fenton Taylor, of New York, a graduate of Harvard in the Class of 1875, and Mary (Stetson) Taylor, originally of Bangor, Maine. His brother, Dr. Fenton Taylor, of New York, graduated at Harvard College in 1909. His own record, in school, college, and the larger world, as provided for the purposes of these memoirs is as follows:

His preparation for college was made at the Newark Academy, Newark, New Jersey, from which he graduated in 1903. He took his part in sports from an early age, and for several years was a member of the school track, baseball, football, basketball, and gymnastic teams.

He entered college in the fall of 1903 and graduated in 1908. His athletic activities in college were numerous. He played on his class football and tennis teams, and in his senior year was substitute quarterback on the varsity football team until serious internal injuries withdrew him from the game. He was a member of the D.K.E., Institute of 1770, Hasty Pudding, and Phoenix Clubs.

On leaving college his desire for active outdoor work caused him to enter the field of contracting. He was associated first with the O'Rourke Engineering Construction Company, working as a pipe-fitter on the Knickerbocker Trust Company's building in New York; then with the Thomas Crimmins Contracting Company; but longest with the T. A. Gillespie Company, all of New York. While with the second of these firms he spent much time on the reconstruction of the barge canal near Rochester, New York, where he made many friends who came into his life later. In the fall of 1913, he established his own contracting company, Taylor, Phillipbrown and Company.

When war broke out in Europe, he decided that individuals, if not the whole country, should be represented in the world's work. Thus it was that as early as September of 1914 he crossed to England and offered his services to the British Red Cross. This organization, through Sir Gregory Jones, sent him with Mrs. Gardner Bartlett to Dieppe where he helped to organize the *Hôpital Anglo-Française No. 37 A*, which had already been started. To this hospital the French government offered a monastery at Yvetot, if the organization at Dieppe could be extended. Since the authorities at No. 37 A felt that they could not do this without help, Taylor was sent to America early in December, 1914, to secure American aid.

At Rochester he secured the services of Dr. Ralph R. Fitch (Harvard, M.D., '03) and his wife. There and in New York he organized committees. Messrs. O'Donnell Iselin (Harvard, '07) and Adrian Devine in Rochester and Lawrence F. Peck (Harvard, '04) in New York joined in this work. The American Red Cross furnished nurses and surgical supplies.

Returning to France Taylor helped to reconstruct the monastery at Yvetot into a sanitary, up-to-date hospital, known officially as the *Hôpital de l'Alliance, Hôpital Auxiliaire du Territoire No. 41 bis*, with accommodations for six hundred patients. Its personnel and funds were half English and half American. When the organization was completed Taylor was made *administrateur général.*

The hospital had good rail and water connections with the war zone, and soon acquired a standing with the French authorities which led to its constant use for seriously wounded cases.

Taylor had a difficult position to fill because of the diverse interests and methods of the French, English, and Americans with whom he had to deal. To his tact and devotion the efficiency of the hospital was in large measure due. Towards the close of the summer of 1915 it was decided to separate the American and English elements into two separate hospitals. Before the time came for engaging in this new work Taylor crossed to England and married Hilda Dancocks, of London, who had been associated with the hospital at Yvetot. Shortly after his marriage, which occurred September 30, he developed mastoiditis, and died at St. Thomas' Hospital, London, on October 19, 1915.

Throughout his short life Taylor displayed, among his chief characteristics, a great fund of energy, common sense, and good fellowship. This was shown both through what he accomplished, and in the host of sincere friends he had made for himself.

One of these, a matron in the hospital at Yvetot wrote on hearing of his death: "I never encountered such a delightfully clean, healthy mind; his judgment of people and situations was remarkable." Another fellow-worker at Yvetot gave fuller expression to the memory he left behind him: "He endeared himself to everyone at the Hospital which he certainly loved and worked for more faithfully than anyone else there. He never deemed any self-sacrifice too great, so long as it might advance the good work of the institution. He was always good-tempered, and usually happy, in spite of a multitude of worries; and it was a joy to see him work out his ideals with a grim determination, and a splendid steadfastness, to their logical conclusion. The splendid work, in this way, which he did in these terrible times, in the cause of human suffering, will always be remembered by us, who esteemed it a privilege to work with him."

ALLEN MACKENZIE CLEGHORN

INSTRUCTOR

DR. CLEGHORN was a Veterinary School Instructor in Comparative Physiology at Harvard in 1899–1900, and Instructor in Physiology in the ensuing year. He was born in London, Ontario, in 1872, of Huguenot, Scotch, Irish, and English ancestry, the son of Andrew Cleghorn. His father's death preceded his own. His mother, his wife, Edna (Gartshore) Cleghorn, and their two children survived him.

After studying as a boy at Trinity College School, Port Hope, Ontario, he attended the University of Toronto, where he received the degree of M.D. in 1892. A term of clinical work as medical superintendent of the Toronto

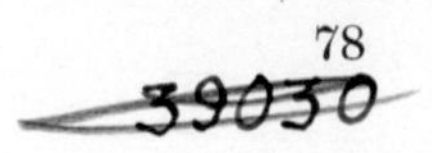

Home for Incurables was followed by the continuance of his medical studies in London, Edinburgh, and Glasgow.

When he came to Harvard in 1899, it was with a background unlike that of his colleagues. A student who has since become a professor in the Medical School recalls him in the following terms: "He was a handsome, dark-haired man of athletic appearance. Experience in Canadian and English medical schools had given him a wide acquaintance with men of his profession. He had also served as a ship physician on liners running to the South Pacific. His wide experience with people of all types and a rather happy memory for amusing situations made him a very agreeable companion, especially when stories were being swapped."

Between 1898 and 1901 he contributed a number of papers on physiological topics to the *American Journal of Physiology*, and one to the *Journal of the Boston Society of Medical Science*. As a teacher he was regarded as "clear, pointed, selective, and sympathetic," and his friendships among students and colleagues were many and genuine.

After two years at the Medical School he took up the practice of his profession in Cambridge. Then his health became impaired, and in the hope of restoring it he returned to Canada, where he spent much time at Algonquin Park, Ontario, fighting off tuberculosis. At the same time he investigated the habits of the wild creatures who were yielding place to civilization, and recorded observations, especially on hibernation, which have since been published. In this period also he prepared a manuscript on racial evolution and eugenics.

When the war came he made repeated solicitations for acceptance by the Royal Army Medical Corps. In December, 1915, his health was considered adequate for field service, and he sailed for England. While awaiting orders to go to the front, with a captain's commission, he contracted broncho-pneumonia, and died March 22, 1916, in the Military Hospital at Bramshott, Hampshire. He was buried at Borden with military honors.

CROSBY CHURCH WHITMAN

Class of 1886

Immediately upon the death of Crosby Church Whitman, in Paris, on March 28, 1916, another graduate of Harvard, William T. Campbell, of the Class of 1875, like Whitman a resident of Paris, but in earlier years a teacher of mathematics in the Adams Academy at Quincy, where Whitman had prepared for college, wrote a memoir of him which tells the essential story of his life and work. It is given herewith:

Dr. Crosby Church Whitman, of the Class of 1886, was born in Benicia, California, March 23, 1863, and died in Paris, France, March 28, 1916. He was the son of Judge Bernard Crosby Whitman and Mary Elizabeth (Church) Whitman. His father, of the Harvard Class of 1846, was a well known attorney-at-law in San

Francisco, and later became Judge of the Supreme Court of Nevada.

Dr. Whitman prepared for college at Adams Academy, Quincy, Massachusetts, where he was a great favorite with both masters and schoolmates. The late Dr. William Everett, headmaster of the Academy, cherished a particular regard for him, and never failed afterwards when visiting Europe to go out of his way to call on him. Every teacher knows that it is one thing for a boy to do well what he likes to do, and quite a different thing if a subject is not to his taste; for then success depends on character. Dr. Whitman was a case in point. He did so well in mathematics that his teacher, knowing that he came from a section of the country where science would be in special demand, supposed he was preparing to follow some branch of engineering; it was only after entering college that he said he had no taste for mathematics and had never thought of taking up a profession where they would be the foundation.

In college his relaxation was in music. He was a very good pianist and his services were in constant demand for the musical entertainments of the societies to which he belonged. Early in the course he was chosen pianist for the Pierian Sodality, of which later he became secretary. He was a member of the D.K.E., librarian of the Institute of 1770, and president and musical director of the Hasty Pudding Club. He was graduated at Harvard with the degree of A.B., but his medical education was acquired in Paris where he was admitted to the *Doctorat en Médecine.*

After an interval of experience in New York, returning to Paris, Dr. Whitman began his life work of private practice and of public services of various kinds originating in the American Hospital at Neuilly, of which he was one of the founders. He was occupied in this way when the war broke out. On the approach of the Germans he made it his first duty to secure the safety of his patients. He was then invited by Mr. James H. Hyde, of the Harvard Class of 1898, to organize an ambulance in his residence, to be placed under the flag of the *Croix Rouge Française*. He took up this work with enthusiasm, and was appointed *médecin chef* by the Minister of War; all was ready when the wounded arrived from the Battle of the Marne.

With unfailing courtesy to all whom he met, and the many qualities which have endeared him to his friends, he devoted himself to his new duties, soothing sufferers by words as well as by professional skill, encouraging the despondent, and frequently providing at his personal expense the best apparatus for unfortunate amputated men when the time came for them to leave the ambulance. In the multiplicity of details, many annoyances were inevitable; but he always kept his cheerful serenity; it was said that a mere glance at his countenance was enough to make a wounded man feel sure that he was on the road to recovery.

Some months afterwards, when Mr. James Stillman placed his residence at the disposition of the *Hôpital Militaire du Val-de-Grace*, Dr. Whitman organized this ambulance, also, and was appointed *médecin chef* by the medical director of Val-de-Grace, retaining his former duties and having the additional responsibility that the new ambulance was reserved for officers, some of high rank. It is needless to say that the care of two ambulances was a serious strain; besides this he was on the staff of the Franco-Belge Dispensary for the relief of refugees from the war zone, and he visited nearly every day an ambulance established in the *École Polytechnique;* but he was so happy and successful in the work that he felt no fatigue.

It was during January, 1916, on the first relaxation of pressure in the ambulances of Paris, that he felt the magnitude of his effort. On the advice of his associates he interrupted his work, as he supposed, for a few days; but his health failed rapidly. He passed away in his sleep, at his own residence in Paris, in the presence of his mother, the household, and the attending physicians.

Throughout the war his ashes remained in a chapel in Paris, whence his mother planned to transfer them to California. They have been buried, instead, in the Suresnes Cemetery, a plot of ground in Paris given by the French Government for the burial of American officers and men, fallen in the war.

His patients in the ambulances came from all classes and all branches of the service. Letters received from men who returned to the front or to their homes breathe affection and gratitude. One cannot say which class was the most impressed with his personality — the Algerian *tirailleurs*, the French soldiers, or the officers of high rank.

He was a dutiful son, a loyal friend, and a devoted physician.

To this narrative and estimate a few facts, drawn chiefly from Reports of the Class of 1886, should be added. On graduating at Harvard College, Whitman's first plan was to study law, and his name appears on the roll of the Harvard Law School for the year of 1886–87. But his real occupation from 1886 to 1895, according to his own record of his life, was the study of medicine in France and Germany. Much travel, in all parts of Europe, fell also within these years. In 1894 he took his medical degree at the University of Paris, and in 1895 returned to the United States. For two years, until 1897, he served as first assistant to Dr. Osler at Johns Hopkins University. In 1898 he took up private practice in New York. His health then failed him, and in 1901 he wrote in a Class Report: "I should like to have a word with all those who smile and say neurasthenia doesn't amount to much." In 1901 he went to Paris and became medical director in charge of the Paris office of the Equitable Life Insurance Company, besides engaging in private practice. In 1908 he was appointed physician to the New American Hospital of Paris in Neuilly.

Of the place he made for himself in Paris, his friend Henry W. Hardon, of New York, of the Harvard Class of

1882, wrote soon after his death: "His uncommonly attractive personal qualities made friends of all his acquaintances. His unusual skill met with ready recognition. He had speedily a position really unique in Paris, where his services were demanded by Frenchmen as well as by foreigners. In the American community he had acquired an influential position." [1]

This friend wrote further of Whitman: "About a year ago I made the rounds of his hospital with him. 'Courage, mon ami! Ça va déjà mieux. Encore un peu de temps et vous verrez. Tenez! Y-a-t-il quelque chose que vous voulez? J'ai écrit à votre mère. Elle va venir.' — 'Merci, docteur; rien pour le moment. Mais que vous êtes bon!'

"Que vous êtes bon! — Who can say that Whitman, '86, has missed a career of great distinction?"

[1] See *Harvard Alumni Bulletin,* May 17, 1916.

MERRILL STANTON GAUNT

Andover 1914–16

Merrill Stanton Gaunt was a graduate of Amherst, in the class of 1914, who came to Harvard in the autumn of that year to study for the ministry at the Andover Theological Seminary. After the mid-year examinations in the winter of 1916, he sailed, February 16, for France to enter the ambulance service. He was sent immediately to the Verdun front with Section 5 of the Norton-Harjes Unit, and after a few weeks of dangerous service, died, April 3, 1916, of cerebro-spinal meningitis in hospital at Bar-le-Duc, where he was buried with French military honors.

He was born in Burrillville, Rhode Island, July 12, 1892, the son of Henry and Mary L. Gaunt. Methuen, Massachusetts, became the home from which he went, in due course, to Worcester Academy, Amherst, and Harvard. A schoolmate at Methuen and Worcester, who was also with him at Amherst, has described his most marked characteristics as enthusiasm and determination. He was a hard worker, rather than a brilliant student, in college, accomplishing what he set out to do, including the playing of football and hockey on his class teams. He was a member of the Amherst chapter of the Chi Psi Fraternity. In the summer of 1912 he worked his way to Europe on a cattle steamer, and was influenced toward socialism by what he saw of the life of the British sailors. In the following summer, in order to inform himself more fully regarding that life, he shipped as a cook on a freighter to South America. He did not decide to enter the ministry till after leaving Amherst. In his single summer vacation, while studying at the Andover Seminary, he did missionary work in South Dakota, covering four small towns on horseback. In term-time at Harvard he managed boys' clubs in Waltham and Watertown, and was in charge of eleven such clubs in Roxbury. He also did settlement work in Boston, and was a director of the Alumni Social Service Bureau in that city. He was a member of the Cosmopolitan Club of Harvard, and of the International Socialist Club.

The school and college friend already cited sailed with him as a steerage passenger on the *Adriatic*, a few days after the group of Harvard and other volunteers for the ambulance service which they were to join sailed on a steamer of the French line. This friend relates that among the steerage passengers were many families of Canadian soldiers going to Europe to be near their men on leave, and that Gaunt made friends with many of them, whose passage he cheered by playing the piano and in other ways. He made also an enemy of the purser of the ship by opening the port-hole in his stateroom, when the officers would not open the ventilators. This brought him and his comrade under suspicion as spies, with the result that they had to report at Scotland Yard on every day of their stay in London, on the way to Paris, pending the investigation of their credentials. From Paris they went to the front within a few days, arriving there early in March, at the height of the First Battle of Verdun, in which they saw immediate and exhausting service. Gaunt devised a new way of hanging blankets in the ambulance, which so commended itself to his superior officer that he insisted upon its general adoption. For the nature of the service in which Gaunt bore his brief part and won the *Croix de Guerre*, a General Order of the 11th French Army, signed by General Pétain, April 3, 1916, making the following citation of Section 5 of the Norton-Harjes Ambulance Unit, speaks with sufficient clearness. This unit, it says:

> . . . a assuré pendant une période de onze jours de combat, du 8 au 19 mars, avec un mépris absolu du danger, les évacuations dans une zone particulièrement battue par l'artillerie ennemie. De plus, tout son personnel a fait preuve d'un dévouement et d'une endurance remarquables en assurant, par un service moyen de 19 heures par jour, le maximum de rendement de cette unité.

One of Gaunt's instructors in the Andover Seminary has recalled his lively interest in social service, and has said: "It was the humane rather than the speculative or scholastic view from which he prepared for the ministry. He was a boy with a keen sense of human need and a very lovable mixture of scientific and romantic interest in trying to help it." The principal of the Worcester Academy during Gaunt's term of study there, Dr. D. W. Abercrombie, of the Harvard Class of 1876, has written of him more fully, as follows:

I found him singularly unaffected and genuine. There was a rare reticence that marked the sincerity of his nature, as if he should say "don't expect many words from me, let what I am about disclose what I am." And he was busy about many things, always "consuming his own smoke," making no declarations, but finding his best self-expression in what he was doing, not in what he was saying. There was a look of determination on his characterful face and in his quiet eyes that showed the power to arrive at the point proposed.

He counted for much in his community by weight of character and by resoluteness of purpose. His life even as an Academy boy seemed an ordered life in its aims and in its methods as well. He had no thought for himself, and, apparently was clear in his mind of the ways and means by which his purposes were to be achieved.

He had a real interest in the school, in its student activities, as well as in his studies. Weighing less than the average fellow who tried for the football team, he was very regular and faithful in being on the field in his suit ready and eager to go where sent. He stood up against the regular eleven when many a fellow of greater weight and strength did not. So he proved by his spirit that he wished to be a good citizen as far as was in his power, contributing all he had to the community to which he belonged.

MERRILL STANTON GAUNT

In the finest sense of the word he was a *socialist.* Socialism was at the core of that sheaf of purposes he lived and died for. The spiritual content of the strong Latin word *socius* animated and armed him, and sent him into that life of self-sacrifice to which he literally gave his life. School patriotism, a college career at Amherst, preparation for the Christian ministry at Harvard, life as a true minister of Christ in the ambulance service in France were simply the successive steps in the career his heart had determined on in the quiet student days at school and college. Would there were no lower form of socialism! The "one clear call" came to him under circumstances that proved the beauty of the purpose of his life. He could show his love for his fellow men in no nobler way than he did in laying down his life for his fellows.

After Gaunt's death the Worcester Academy sent an ambulance to France, dedicated to his memory. A bronze tablet placed in Andover Hall by his classmates in the Andover Theological Seminary and Harvard Divinity School shows his fine profile in relief, and commemorates him in the following terms:

MERRILL STANTON GAUNT
CLASS OF 1917
ANDOVER THEOLOGICAL SEMINARY
HARVARD DIVINITY SCHOOL
MDCCCXCII–MCMXVI
VOLUNTEER AMERICAN AMBULANCE CORPS
DIED IN SERVICE AT BAR-LE-DUC IN FRANCE
ON APRIL 3RD
AWARDED THE CROIX DE GUERRE
A LOVER OF MEN AN ADVOCATE OF PEACE
A BELOVED FELLOW-STUDENT
A SERVANT OF THE KINGDOM OF GOD

VICTOR EMMANUEL CHAPMAN

Class of 1913

A remarkable volume, "Victor Chapman's Letters from France," contains a memoir of this young man by his father, John Jay Chapman, of the Harvard Class of 1884, a biography in little which must be counted, now and hereafter, as one of the memorable pieces of writing evoked by the war. The attempt of the following paragraphs will be primarily to draw enough from the book of his letters, with his father's explications, to tell the essential story of the life and death of this first American aviator who gave his life for France — and perhaps to send some readers to the book itself.

Victor Emmanuel Chapman was born in New York City, April 17, 1890. In his father's blood there was a vital strain of the New England abolitionist of the mid-nineteenth century; in that of his mother (Minna Timmins, half-Italian, half-American) a Latin fervor, producing a blend of inheritances from which the more usual qualities of young Americans could hardly have been expected to emanate. In Victor Chapman there seems always to have been something unusual — a capacity of brooding sorrow, quickened by the early death of his mother, a strong religious sense, carried from childhood through boyhood into manhood, a zeal for righteousness, a love for danger so positive that much of the best in him lay dormant until the provocation of peril stirred him into activity, a corresponding love for natural scenery and for animals, a devotion to younger brothers and to friends, especially when they needed him, that had a quality of knighthood in it. There was also much that was ungainly, inarticulate, and slowly maturing in both the boy and the man. Nearly all of these points are illustrated by concrete instances recalled by Chapman's father. Soon after his death a classmate told this characteristic story: "Just five and a half years ago, I think, Chapman declined to follow me across some ice floes half a mile out to sea because the going was palpably unsafe, and inside of ten minutes he had saved my life by returning and walking out to sea till he finally hooked me out from the icy water on the muzzle end of a loaded and cocked rifle. Nothing could be more typical of him."

Such an one he had already shown himself in college. His preparation for it was made at the Fay School, Southborough, St. Paul's School, Concord, in France and Germany for a year, and at the Stone School in Boston for his final year of schooling. He had no aptitude for sports, said his father, nor for books; and the passion for color and scenery which offset these lacks was not a gift to make him at all a conspicuous figure in the college community. A letter of his own, after he had begun to fly in France, suggests at least one of his undergraduate pleasures: "It is easier to pilot an aeroplane than drive an auto when you get on, and far less dangerous than the autoing I used to do daily at Cambridge." By ways of his own he was developing a force of character in keeping with the largeness and strength of his body.

On graduating from College in 1913 he went immediately to Paris and entered an atelier for the preliminary studies in architecture which he was to pursue at the Beaux-Arts. He had thus been in France for about a year when the war began. It had lasted hardly more than a month when he volunteered for service in the Foreign Legion of the French Army, and was accepted.

For nearly a year he remained in the Legion, serving in the trenches at a point, as his father says, "where there were no attacks, but where inaction and the continual 'sniping' severely tried the nerves. Kohn, an accomplished Polish mathematician was shot, as he and Victor were leaning over the *talus*. He died in Victor's arms. For over one hundred consecutive days Victor was in the front trenches as *aide-chargeur* to a *mitrail.* He was slightly wounded once, and one-half of his squadron were either killed or seriously hurt." Through all this service he displayed the greatest cheerfulness in the performance of extremely miscellaneous tasks, the truest human kindness to his comrades, and an unfailing courage. The Legion, as Henry Farnsworth's letters have shown, brought together the most diverse types of men. In one of Chapman's letters a few of them pass in review:

It might be of interest to you to know the names of the men in my squad. Markus, better class Russian Pole with French wife; Herédia, Malaga Spanish, writes for Spanish papers and has translated Mark Twain, etc.; Held, Swiss origin, born in Paris; Gabai, Turkish Jew, Constantinople, Spanish ancestry, cheap *chemisier;* Millet, Italian from near Monaco; Zimmermann, Alsatian, Strassburg, professional bicyclist, served as orderly to officer in Germany, speaks French with a vile accent; Zudak, Russian Pole, very greedy, speaks considerable French; Chikechki, ditto, speaks better French, a strong fellow; Bogdan, Austrian Pole, no French but German; Canbrai, miner, simple man, never gives trouble; Bajteck, Austrian Pole, greedy. These Poles are by far the best material physically for soldiers; and though not very bright, they do not give trouble. Gabai, the Turk, is all the time talking and getting into most heated arguments whenever anyone will talk to him, in fact, his presence is always felt when he is in the room by his constant flow of language. Manchiuski, the slight little Pole tailor, calls him the *mitrailleuse.* Recently Held got himself changed to the kitchen; the reason he gave me was that he could not stand the constant yelling and cursing.

Victor Chapman had not been in the Legion a month when he related the following incident, with its unconscious revelation of what he was beginning to mean to his companions in arms:

> I made a sentimental *faux-pas* at Reuilly Caserne one night. It was after taps but the lamp was still burning. I lay trying to sleep with my head to the middle of the room. In fact I was almost asleep. There was a call in the room. I afterwards learned that the unfortunate Germans were called to be sent to Morocco. Some one said, "*Où est* Chapman?" and the next thing I knew some one embraced me. I thought it was some joke, and lifting my leg pushed him across the room. A voice whimpered "*Sans blague, c'est adieu.*" It was a poor fellow I had seen a few times, who, though really French, was born in Germany and had put his name down as German. Then he hurried off, but I was much touched by his kiss for I hardly knew him and never heard his name.

A fellow *Légionnaire* has told another story, of significance:

> One day a *mitrailleur* came up to him saying, "I'm sick. The major has ordered me to drink milk for two weeks; but there isn't any here. They're going to send me to the rear, and I'm bored with the notion." "Good," said Victor. "Stay where you are; I'll settle it." At dinner time Chapman disappeared. That evening the section saw him returning accompanied by a cow which he was dragging behind him. "I bought her so that you could get your milk," said he to the sick *mitrailleur*. "Now you can stay with us." Chapman was the Maecenas of the regiment, the master of revels, the friend of all.

Much of the life in the trenches was tedious in the extreme to Victor Chapman. He "kept himself going," perhaps most of all, through interest in the human beings about him. Occasional meetings with Alan Seeger and Henry Farnsworth were noted with pleasure. "I go to see

Farnsworth daily" — he wrote, April 12, 1915 — "and catch myself making estimates as to how he keeps up his interest . . . I must say I come back feeling gayer after seeing him." He turned for comfort also to books — Lamb, the Autocrat, Hamlet, Galsworthy, Emerson, a new volume of his father's, read with pride and delight, the Bible. He made water-color sketches, with an increasingly skilful hand, when he could, and betrayed the architect's eye by comments, in his letters, upon the ruined buildings of Northern France. He saw the beauties of nature about him: "Apple trees are now in bloom," he wrote in May of 1915, "and when the nights are not too windy birds chirp all through them. I have not yet, however, heard anything to resemble my conception of a nightingale's voice. Last night, after the disturbing influence of the artillery, both sides sent up occasional rockets, short flickering stars which rose, bobbed a moment, and went out, showing up only the black silhouette of trees and feathery clouds banked upon one another. Did I tell you that in my night watches I have taken particular interest in the stars? — like the ancient shepherds, — and have made some shrewd guesses as to the Zodiac constellations."

In spite of all these interests the comparatively inactive lot which happened to befall Chapman in the Legion became most irksome to him. "The boring part of this life" — he wrote to his father in February, 1915 — "is that it is only ideal for a boy of fifteen. Constructing houses without boards; camping out with its hardships and difficulties to be overcome; generally living a happy-go-lucky, hand-to-mouth existence; losing things right and left, if they are abundant; — I have lost, I fear, almost entirely my perspective of the outside world." A few months later, while still in the Legion, he wrote: "I feel that this is a most excellent apprenticeship for the job of tending a light-house or light-ship. At first when the place is new, the work is interesting, the events (storms, etc.) are exciting; then one loses more and more the outside point of view. The fine sunsets and sunrises get monotonous, the people one thought picturesque and amusing at first sight, lose their interest, and you have recourse to books, magazines, and newspapers. Of course here I do a little more. Give English lessons, for instance." As time wore on, Chapman became more and more disgusted with having "neither helped the French, nor injured the Germans," as he put it, and when the opportunity came to join the Lafayette Escadrille of American aviators in the French Army, a *corps d'élite* organized by Norman Prince (Harvard, '08), Frazier Curtis (Harvard, '98), and Elliot C. Cowdin (Harvard, '09), he seized it with avidity. His only regret appears to have been that he was not with it from its very inception.

"Victor's entry into the American Aviation was, to him," says his father, "like being made a Knight. It transformed — one might almost say — transfigured him. That the universe should have supplied this spirit with the consummation which it had sought from infancy and should have given, in a few weeks, complete happiness and complete fulfillment, — the crown of a life to which one can imagine no other perfect ending, — is one of the mysteries of this divine age." In August, 1915, his transfer to the Aviation Corps was effected. Then followed months of training, first as *mitrailleur* or *bombardier*, then as *piloto*. A graphic letter of August 25, describes his first successful raid into Germany, and his own joy at seeing the aerial bomb which he launched land on a railroad track, and not on civilian houses. In the spring he was ready to go to the front, and May 23 he wrote from Verdun: "We are really settling down to work, and I begin to feel that I am actively saving France and no longer toying with her expensive utensils." How much of a game it still was the following paragraph from a letter of June 1 will tell:

This morning we all started off at three, and, not having made concise enough arrangements, got separated in the morning mist. I found Prince, however, and we went to Douaumont where we found two German *reglagé* machines unprotected and fell upon them. A skirmish, a spitting of guns, and we drew away. It had been badly executed, that manoeuvre. But ho! Another Boche heading for Verdun! Taking the direction stick between my knees I tussled and fought with the *mitrailleuse* and finally charged the *rouleau*, all the while eyeing my Boche and moving across Vaux towards Étain. I had no altitude with which to overtake him, but a little more speed. So I got behind his tail and spit till he dived into his own territory. Having lost Norman, I made a tour to the Argonne and on the way back saw another fat Boche. "No protection machine in sight." I swooped, swerved to the right, to the left, almost lost, but then came up under his lee keel by the stern. (It's the one position they cannot shoot from.) I seemed a dory alongside a schooner. I pulled up my nose to let him have it. Crr-Crr-Crr — a cartridge jammed in the barrel. He jumped like a frog and fled down to his grounds. Later in the morning I made another stroll along the lines. Met a flock of Nieuports, and saw across the way a squad of white-winged L. V. G. How like a game of prisoner's base it all is! I scurry out in company, and they run away. They come into my territory and I being alone, take to my heels. They did come after me once too! Faster they are than I, but I had height so they could but leer up at me with their dead-white wings and black crosses like sharks, and they returned to their own domain.

In this and other letters there are vivid little pictures of the scenes that constantly gave pleasure to his eyes. "Everyone says they get tired of flying. 'It's monotonous.' I don't see it," he wrote on June 5, continuing,

but on the contrary, an infinite variety is this, when there is a slight sprinkling of clouds. Clouds are not thin pieces of blotting paper; but liquid, ceaselessly changing steam. I played hide-and-seek in and out them yesterday; sometimes flat blankets like melting snow on either side below me, or again, like great ice floes with distant bergs looming up, and "open water" near at hand, blue as a moonstone cloud, floating full, for all the world like a gigantic jelly-fish (those that have red trailers and a sting). In the nearer pools the mottled earth, piebald with sun and shadow, showed through; and it was thanks to these I knew my whereabouts. I was going from below the clouds to above them, circling in some hole; thus I realized the size and thickness of the walls, — 300 metres sheer from top to base of dazzling whiteness. Some have many feathery, filmy points and angles, others are rounded and voluminous, with cracks and caverns in them. These are all the fair-weather, fleecy clouds; for there are the lower, flatter, misty ones, and the speckled, or mare's tail clouds, above which one never reaches. There are such a lot of trumpet-shaped and wind-blown clouds this evening that I should like to go out and examine them; but it's a bore for my mechanic, and I doubt if I could go high enough to warrant crossing the lines.

The *gaudium certaminis* was joined with all of Chapman's enjoyment of beauty, for he was constantly in combat with German machines, and landing with injuries to himself and his plane, yet eager to take wing again at the earliest opportunity. It irked him greatly not to be constantly at it — seeing clearly at the same time the humors of the notice his exploits were attracting. Only a few weeks before his death he wrote:

> It seems an exceptional chance for getting into the public eye, though, I must say it's too bad I'm not going into politics after the war so that I could make use of all this free advertising. I might almost run for the Assembly so as not to lose such a golden opportunity. Anyway, Conrad and Chanler [his younger brothers] are benefiting. I take it they will be pointed out at the Military Camps: "Hist! Dat guy has a brudder in the real war. He kills Chermans every mornin' like sparrers." Meanwhile, I sit in an open window with waves of leaden clouds drifting by, and the indefatigable graphophone churns out some vulgar tune below, and the other "heroes" play poker, and the Captain practises scales on the piano. It is disintegrating to mind and body, — this continued inertia.

The inertia was never of long continuance, or other than under compulsion, as it was at this very time, because of a head wound received in action. A few days later a fellow-member of the Escadrille, Clyde Balsley, was wounded and taken to a hospital behind Verdun. Before long it was found that champagne or oranges would hasten his recovery. Chapman at once made provision for the champagne, and, as soon as he was permitted to fly again himself, began taking oranges to his friend. This he designed to do on the day of his death, June 23, 1916. Indeed the basket of oranges was placed in the machine in which he followed his captain, Thenault, Norman Prince, and Raoul Lufbery, when they set forth to go over the lines early in the afternoon. Chapman's purpose was to fly after them for a time, and then land at the hospital with the oranges for Balsley. But the captain, Prince, and Lufbery, seeing and attacking two German planes, were soon attacked by two or three more, turning the odds against them. Chapman saw the situation, and rushed into the fight, unseen by his three friends, who believing themselves hopelessly outnumbered, started for their own lines. The reversed odds were now hopeless indeed — four or five against one. That one was seen — not by his own comrades, who supposed all the while that he was visiting his friend in hospital, but by quite another observer — to dash to the ground, with his machine at full speed and uncontrolled. This report did not reach the Escadrille for a week after the event. "A glorious death" — wrote Norman Prince when the news came — "*face à l'ennemi* and for a great cause and to save a friend!"

From an unexpected angle Victor Chapman may be seen only a few days before his epical death — at the bedside of Clyde Balsley in the hospital at Vatlincourt. This glimpse of him appears in a narrative, "'Severely Wounded,' The Story of a Wounded American in a French Hospital, Transcribed by Ruth Dunbar," which was printed in the *Century Magazine* for February, 1919. It is Balsley's own story, in which, after describing his intense longing for water, as he lay, greatly suffering, in the hospital, he says:

So violent was this one longing that I was actually blinded. I did not at first see a man standing beside my bed.

They came to me one by one — the heavy, black hair, the great arms, and the sincerest eyes in the world. When I put them all together, I gave a groan of joy. It was Victor Chapman, flown over from Bar-le-Duc.

"Hello, old boy," he was saying. "Here's your tooth-brush."

He was holding it out in his great paw, and I think I realized even then how hard he was trying to be matter-of-fact. The tooth-brush, the English words, the dear American voice, the aviator whom every one in our squad loved deeply — I knew nothing now except that I had them again. Then in a moment it came back to me, the terrible thirst. "Oh," I thought, with a touch of the craftiness that is part of sickness, "if I can only *look* how thirsty I am, Vic will do something about it. He'll see that I get something better than an old wet bandage to suck."

"Anything I can get for you, old man?" said he, meeting my thirsty eyes.

"You bet," said I. "They won't let me have any water." The way I kept moistening my lips finished the appeal.

"How about oranges?" said he, and turned to my doctor, just at that moment come in.

"*Bien*," answered the surgeon, with a shrug; "but there are not any to be had in the village."

"Guess we'll fix that," said Victor. "I'll get you those oranges if I have to fly to Paris."

I looked from one to the other. Oranges! Why hadn't I thought of those before? There is a certain sublime ignominy in the way a sick man permits himself to gloat over something which he cannot have. I gave myself up to this ignominy completely.

"Don't you worry," said Victor, lingering by my side and giving my arm a bearlike pat. "Be out of this in no time."

He was part of my beloved Bar-le-Duc, he was my friend in a world of strangers.

The oranges came, as we have seen, until, one near day, they were brought by another than Victor Chapman, and Balsley learned that this friend would come no more.

A funeral service for Victor Chapman was held in the American Church at Paris on July 4 — a happy accident of date which gave the occasion a remarkable international significance. "America has sent us this sublime youth," wrote a French woman, "and our gratitude for him is such that it flows back upon his country. Wherever I go I am asked about him. Never since the outbreak of the war has public sentiment been more deeply aroused."

On May 24 Victor Chapman had been proposed for sergeant and for the *Croix de Guerre*. The papers were passed, and reached the Escadrille two days after his death; but Chapman learned on the morning of his last flight that they were coming. The *Médaille Militaire* would also have reached him in July had the necessary papers been signed, according to rule, before his death. The following citation appeared in the *Journal Officiel* for October 7, 1916:

> Chapman (Victor) sergent pilote à l'escadrille N. 124: pilote de chasse qui était un modèle d'audace, d'énergie et d'entrain et faisait l'admiration de ses camarades d'escadrille. Sérieusement blessé à la tête le 17 juin, a demandé à ne pas interrompre son service. Quelques jours plus tard, s'étant lancé à l'attaque de plusieurs avions ennemis, a trouvé une mort glorieuse au cours de la lutte.

At Harvard the "Victor Emmanuel Chapman Memorial Fellowship" for the maintenance of a French youth as a student in the University preserves his name to future generations.

CLYDE FAIRBANKS MAXWELL

CLASS OF 1914

THE son of a British subject, Walter Maxwell, A.M. (Harvard) 1889, Government Inspector of sugar refineries in New South Wales, Clyde Fairbanks Maxwell was born in Northampton, Massachusetts, April 14, 1892. His mother, Annie (Weber) Maxwell was an American, but this son, though ardently American in feeling, never became a citizen of the United States, as it is believed he would have done had he survived the war. Through his boyhood in the Antipodes he attended school at Armidale and Sydney, New South Wales. While he was a pupil at the Armidale School, it is related that on one occasion, after the military cadets of the school had saluted the British colors, Clyde Maxwell produced an American flag and, spreading the stars and stripes to the breeze, called out "Now, boys, I'll show you something worthy of your honor." The young colonials fortunately took it all in good part, gave the cheer for which the half-American hoped, and thenceforth called him "Doodles."

Coming to Harvard quite without friends in the College, he soon made them there. Soccer was the only college sport he knew, and as a freshman he became a substitute on the Harvard Soccer Team. Besides, he rowed on crews, dormitory and other, joined the Western Club, and held an associate editorship of the *Harvard Illustrated.* His scholastic standing won him at the same time a Harvard College Scholarship in both his sophomore and his senior year, which was for him a half-year, at the end of which he completed the studies entitling him to a bachelor's degree.

The war began hardly more than a month after the graduation of Maxwell's class. He sailed at once for England and entered training as an infantry officer. When his regiment, the Ninth Essex, was about to start for the front, the condition of his health obliged him to ask for sick leave. This lasted for a year, in the course of which he became engaged to be married. Early in June, 1916, he joined his regiment in France, a Lieutenant. His service at the front was ended by death in action about a month later. His father has described the final scene:

Concerning the fact and circumstances of the death of Lieutenant Clyde F. Maxwell, the following is the nearest to exactness that I can furnish. I will remark that Lieutenant Maxwell was reported as missing, and it was some nine months later that the fact and circumstances of his end were furnished by one of the wounded but surviving men whom Lieutenant Maxwell led into action.

The Ninth Essex Infantry went into action at dawn on the morning of July 3, 1916, at La Boisselle. Lieutenant Clyde F. Maxwell was wounded during the first half-hour, and should have retired. As ranking officer of his platoon, he declined to retire out of action, and led on his men. Near the end of the fourth hour of the action he was mortally wounded. The private soldier, who is authority for this account, stated that after Lieutenant Maxwell was struck the second time by shell he was unable to rise, or to speak, but by the motion of his uninjured arm he urged forward his men. Shortly after his fall he rolled into a shell hole and was "blown in" by a further shell, the exact place being unknown now.

I may add the following: Young officers when going into action frequently placed in the most convenient pocket of their uniform an open, but addressed envelope containing a blank sheet of paper, with an attached pencil. It appears that Lieutenant Maxwell had made this provision, as a closed letter was found in, or near, the German trench which his platoon had taken. The letter was forwarded to the address in England that the envelope bore. It was received by a young girl friend of Lieutenant Maxwell. He had not been able to do more than take out of his uniform the letter and close it — with blood. The enclosed sheet was blank.

The receipt of that letter indicated the end of Lieutenant Maxwell; yet it was only after some nine months that the indication was confirmed.

The Commanding Officer of the Regiment communicated to his family a statement of the coolness and great heroism of Lieutenant Maxwell during action previous to his fall.

"Pater, you know I must make good" were the last words he had said to his father before leaving England. This he did, in a manner amply justifying the characterization of him in the Second Report of the Class of 1914: "Maxwell was a man of the highest ideals, very modest and unassuming, with a sense of duty which would brook no shirking. Those whom he called friends were always warm friends, and these he never failed and never lost."

ALAN SEEGER

CLASS OF 1910

BECAUSE Alan Seeger was a writer, and a writer who commanded serious attention, there is ample material for a more detailed memoir of him than this can possibly be. A thorough treatment of the subject would involve a careful study of origins and influences, ancestral and individual, with special reference to the more formative years of the young poet's life. Here it must suffice to give the essential facts of his brief but fruitful career, drawing freely upon words of his own to record his attitude towards life and some of his dealings with it.

He was born in New York, June 22, 1888, the son of Charles Louis Seeger, and Elsie (Adams) Seeger. The fact that a part of his boyhood was spent in Mexico, where his father had business interests and sometimes lived, taken together with his somewhat exotic appearance, due to picturesque clothing and a conspicuous mat or thatch of black hair, gave the impression in College that his strangeness was something racial and complete. As a matter of fact his blood was chiefly that of New England, and except for the few years in Mexico, with its many cosmopolitan influences, his vacations in the New Hampshire hills, and a winter in Southern California, his boyhood was subjected to influences no more remote than those of New York City, Staten Island, and Tarrytown, New York, where he was prepared at Hackley School to enter Harvard College. Yet all these spots were spots of beauty — places in which the eye might take a various delight and school itself to the uses of art in whatever form. Especially of the poet it may be said: "As what he sees is, so have his thoughts been."

The poet and the child have this in common, that they are continually passing through "phases." In college Seeger passed through the alternate phases of loathing and loving the whole thing. In the second stage, his mother has written, "he was in perfect despair over having wasted those years, and not entered more into the life there." Writing of this time in the final year of his own life he said of it, "I was a devotee of Learning for Learning's sake.

My life during those years was intellectual to the exclusion of almost everything else. The events of that life were positive adventures to me. Few, I am sure, have known more than I did then the employ of intellect as an instrument of pleasure. I shut myself off completely from the life of the University, so full, nevertheless, of pleasures. I scoffed at these pleasures that were no more to me than froth. I felt no need of comradeship. I led the life of an anchorite. At an age when the social instincts are usually most lively I came to understand the pleasures of solitude. My books were my friends. The opening to me of the shelves of the college library, a rare privilege, was like opening the gates of an earthly paradise. In those dark alleys I would spend afternoons entire, browsing among old folios, following lines of research that often had no connection with my courses, following them simply for the pleasure of the explorer discovering new countries. I never regret those years. They made their contribution. Their pleasures were tranquil and pure. Their desires were simple and all the means of satisfying them were at hand."

With these student years of delving into obscure books it is interesting to associate the possible origin of the phrase a "rendezvous with death," which is the core of Seeger's poem best known throughout the world. In "The Advance of English Poetry in the Twentieth Century," by Professor Phelps of Yale, there is quoted a letter from Professor Robinson of Harvard telling of the strong impression made upon Seeger by the Irish "Song of Fothad Canainne," which he read in a Celtic Conference, a song which sings: "It is a blindness for one who makes a tryst to set aside the tryst with death." The phrase which Seeger stamped so clearly with his own mintage has been ascribed by others to other sources. But it is certainly plausible that the echo of the early Irish singer may have still rung in the ears of the soldier of the Legion who had once been a student in Harvard College.

The following passages from two letters which Seeger wrote from Mexico in the summer vacation of 1909 to his friend and classmate, Edward Eyre Hunt, show how clearly conscious of his poetic ambitions Seeger was even before his college years were done:

4a de Humboldt 42, City of Mexico, Mex.
August 21, 1909.

Dear Hunt:

... My purpose in writing you again so soon is a tentative one; I should like to have your opinion on an idea that occurred to me a while ago. Now I suppose all of us who are at present devoting ourselves to poetical expression, "scorning delights and living laborious days," are doing so with the intention sooner or later of collecting what seem to us the best of our productions and publishing them as a first venture. It goes without saying that individually we already have a certain amount of accomplishment that seems fit for such a collection, though perhaps not enough of the best to form a volume. But I thought, why would it not be a pleasant thing if a half-dozen or so of us should combine what seemed to us the best of our work of this kind, which is also too long for the common standard of the college papers, and publish it in a single volume, as the achievement of the best talent of the Class of 1910? And not only this, but call it Vol. I, and affix to it a preface, stating the nature and purpose of the work, and expressing the hope that it be continued in ensuing years. Would not this be something like the Musenalmanachs of German Romanticism? The advantages of the plan seem to me to be these: First, and most important, it would undoubtedly procure a much wider circulation, and consequent recognition, of our work than any individual publication would. Secondly, the expense would be mutual, and we would thereby be enabled to issue it according to our own taste, and in fitting style. To ensure a certain amount of circulation and returns, we could resort, if necessary, to prospectus and subscription. Thirdly, it would not preclude the possibility of including the same material in our later collections, should we wish to do so. Fourthly, it would be an inestimable stimulus to serious literary effort among undergraduates, would be an added bond between men of such tastes, and in the event of anything resembling a "school" rising in our midst, this would be its proper organ. As for a host of minor advantages, such as the pleasure of the undertaking, these need not be dwelt upon.

Personally the idea appeals to me strongly. The contributors, as I fancy it, would be solely members of the graduating class, though this need not be insisted on. The work, as I said before, would be the best individual effort of a kind too long for the magazines; its eligibility would be passed on by the majority of those interested.

The problem of finding an audience is much more difficult today than it was a hundred years ago, for today there is practically no public for poetry as there was in those beloved times when sentimental females hung upon the prolific muse of Byron and Moore, and people watched the press with as eager an interest as today they watch the stock-exchange. Indeed, what more thankless undertaking than to publish a volume of verse now-a-days? I should never think of doing so except privately printed. Happy was Keats whose early work was loaded with contumely, compared with the modern bard whose work is simply ignored or else damned with the faint praise of an incompetent reviewer. Revilement is better than total disregard. The Chatterton whom Vigny pictures in his garret is really more fortunate than his present-day counterpart who would not even be able to raise a ripple of excitement on the stagnant waters of modern literary enervation. True, the poet's utterance should be perfectly spontaneous, unpurposive, without a moment's consideration of the world's opinion, its admiration or neglect; and yet even Shelley, I believe, is authority for the discouragement it is to a writer who believes himself possessed of something worth saying, and never an ear to listen. Now this plan I have been speaking of seems to me the best solution, for here we could have at once just the audience we desire. While in a perfectly disinterested way, it appeals to me as the starting of a tradition which would always be a source of delight and might have unthought-of consequences.

If this interests you, impart the idea to some of the other men. Write me too and say what you think of it. . . .

4a de Humboldt 42, City of Mexico,
7–30–09.

Dear Hunt:

. . . I am going to be in an attic down on Ash St.—No. 16 — next year, and I hope you will come around sometime. It has neither heat nor light, except what I can furnish myself, but it has a beautiful view of the eastern sky and is perfectly quiet, which are far more important. Do come around sometime and let us talk over the prospects of the impecunious poet, who hates everything sordid and material, and would prefer a gypsy life to being chained down to an office-desk — in Gaza of the Philistines. You, of course, with your reputation, have, no doubt, plenty of good openings; certainly you could be a "young instructor" for the asking. But as for me . . . well —

forward, tho I canna see,
I guess and fear.

Seeger's entrance into the life of the College through his later years there took the form especially of frequent and extensive contributions of verse to the *Harvard Monthly*. This periodical, no longer extant, was then passing through a time when its young poets were scorning capital letters for the beginning of their lines unless capitals would have been required in prose. Seeger lent himself, probably with enthusiasm, to this *bizarrerie* of print, which disappears even from the verses of undergraduate days included in the volume of "Poems," for there they are, three original pieces of verse placed with the surprisingly mature "Juvenilia" and a Canto of Dante's "Inferno" among the "Translations." It is all the work of an ardent lover of beauty as an end in itself, and possesses to a striking degree that sensuous quality of beauty which marks the whole body of Seeger's poetic writing. This contribution of poetry to the college life of Seeger's undergraduate years was not one that commanded popularity or prominence, but it was the thing he had to give, and he gave it in abundant measure. The value of the gift is much clearer now than it was in 1910.

A college contemporary of Seeger's, John Hall Wheelock, of the Harvard Class of 1908, has told in the anonymous "Point of View" of *Scribner's Magazine* for January, 1917, of Seeger's utter indifference to the usual incentives, even of young poets. Large as his acknowledged output was, he was constantly reputed to be tearing up verses, unseen by his friends, because he had not satisfied himself with them. A publisher who offered to print his poems soon after he left college is said to have received not even so much as a reply. Mr. Wheelock's descriptions of his first and his last meeting with Seeger present something both of the outward and of the inward aspect of the man:

Seeger was of striking appearance. The writer recalls his first glimpse of him at a rather voluble meeting of one of the literary societies at Harvard where both were at that time undergraduates. Tall and rather sparely built, with a pale, but forceful and strangely immobile and mask-like face, straight black hair cut square across the forehead, and remote eyes, he sat through the entire evening in absolute silence, hardly deigning as much as a reply to questions directly put. At first this might have been attributed to either affectation or shyness, but a certain candor coupled with entire self-possession soon eliminated both solutions. On being questioned by a friend at the close of the discussion as to his extraordinary behavior, he announced with entire naturalness that the conversation had not appealed to him, and added that he was by nature not interested in trivial talk. This episode was characteristic of the man and, incredible as it may seem, carried with it no suggestion of conceit or pose.

The final meeting was three or four years later. Thus Mr. Wheelock records it:

I recall now our last talk. It was during the summer before his departure for France in 1912 and on a perfect moon-clear August night. I recall the familiar fatalism that he then gave voice to, the fierce discontent and hunger of the man, as of one who seeks blindly something greater than himself, whereby he may be liberated, through which he may reveal himself, to which he may consecrate and surrender his entire soul. I recall then the sudden realization, new to me at that moment, that for some spirits the every-day pressure of life is not sufficient, the every-day demands of life not large nor heroic enough in their claim. As for death — well, I recall also his favorite Indian phrase, repeated that evening, and which sums up beautifully his own attitude: "Inshallah, Death is a transient thing!"

Between leaving college in 1910 and going to Paris in 1912 Seeger appears to have led what would commonly be regarded as a life of much futility — refusing to "become implicated in any kind of a job," seeming merely, as Mr. Wheelock has expressed it, "well on the way toward becoming a complete dilettante." Seeger himself knew well enough that he was not laying the foundations of the "success" he was wont to scorn. A letter written at this time to a college official with whom he was on terms of friendship contained a curiously revealing and prophetic sentence: "My only salvation will be to die young and to leave some monument which being, if such is possible, more beautiful than the life it commemorates may seem to posterity an only and adequate excuse for that life having been."

A friend of young poets, who saw much of him during this New York period, has written:

Alan was consistently medieval, and although his criticism of any form of art was surprisingly keen he seemed completely ignorant, or, let me say, unconscious of everything that had been written during recent years. I do not think there was any pose about this, and I always remember with amusement a Sunday afternoon when he and B——— both dropped in unexpectedly to supper. One kept asking if I had seen the latest sonnet by so-and-so which was quite worthy of Keats, and the other was quoting from the *Cantique de Soleil* of St. Francis and Claudion's *De Raptu Persephone*. Neither of my guests seemed to have the slightest comprehension of what the other was talking about and the supper was an amusing affair. . . .

We used to think there was nothing human in the boy, but one night when fire engines passed he threw open the window and put out his head, after which we commenced to have hope of him. The fact that he made such a disagreeable impression on many people was due, I think, to his unconscious rudeness. He was a consistent hedonist and if someone who did not seem to him beautiful, either mentally or physically, happened to come in while he was with us he would take a book and read until that person left. Of course his life abroad and particularly his life during the war changed and developed him greatly.

As "a consistent hedonist" Alan Seeger found in Paris through the two years before the war abundant opportunity to bear his part in the *vie de Bohème* which finds its reflections in his "Poems." But this was not all. "In Paris," says Mr. Wheelock,

> he was happier than he had ever been before. He made many congenial friends, and a number of distinguished and even celebrated figures in the world of art and letters were strangely drawn to the silent young American, who accepted this recognition with his usual calm and poise as something quite to be expected. Again, he was said to be writing much, but again made no efforts to publish, and his work was hardly shown even to his closest friends. He was still uncertain of himself and his aims, still waiting for that destiny which he felt every day more clearly and steadfastly was somehow in preparation for him.

Seeger's own account of himself when a "devotee of Learning for Learning's sake" has already been quoted. In the same letter he refers to his apostasy from Learning, his following in the path of those, "obsessed by the burning vision of Happiness," who "left the quiet groves of the Academy and went down into the city in search of it." The immediately ensuing passage from the same letter, written, let us remember, after a year and a half of soldiering, is needed to complete Seeger's portrait of himself:

> It has been the history of many young men, no doubt. But my hedonism, if such it may be called, was not superficial like that of so many, to whom the emotional means only the sexual. I was sublimely consistent. For seeing, in the macrocosm, all Nature revolve about the twin poles of Love and Strife, of attraction and repulsion, so no less in the microcosm of my individual being I saw the emotional life equally divided between these two cardinal principles. The dedication to Love alone, as Ovid pret-

tily confesses his own in more than one elegy, is good as far as it goes, but it only goes half way, and my aspiration was to go all the gamut, to "drink life to the lees." My interest in life was passion, my object to experience it in all rare and refined, in all intense and violent forms. The war having broken out, then, it was natural that I should have staked my life on learning what it alone could teach me. How could I have let millions of other men know an emotion that I remained ignorant of? Could not the least of them, then, talk about the thing that interested me most with more authority than I? You see, the course I have taken was inevitable. It is the less reason to lament if it leads me to destruction. The things one poignantly regrets are those which seem to us unnecessary, which, we think, might have been different. This is not my case. My being here is not an accident. It is the inevitable consequence, as you see, of a direction deliberately chosen.

The summer of 1914 found Seeger in London, where he vainly sought a publisher for his poems. On his way back to Paris, when war became a certainty, he left his manuscript with a printer in Bruges — not the most prudent choice for safe-keeping — expecting soon to reclaim it for publication. On August 20 he left Bruges to enlist in Paris, and on the 24th enlisted in the Foreign Legion. Near the end of the next month he wrote to his mother from Toulouse, where his regiment of the Legion was drilling:

I hope you see the thing as I do and think that I have done well, being without responsibilities and with no one to suffer materially by my decision, in taking upon my shoulders, too, the burden that so much of humanity is suffering under and, rather than stand ingloriously aside when the opportunity was given me, doing my share for the side that I think right.

Gratitude to Paris for all it had meant to him was a powerfully impelling motive. "To me the matter of supreme importance," he wrote in his diary after nearly a year in the army, "is not to be on the winning side, but on the side where my sympathies lie. . . . Let it always be understood that I never took arms out of any hatred against Germany or the Germans, but purely out of love for France." In another place the motive is given a little differently in Seeger's own accounting for the young volunteers of foreign birth who rushed to the French colors:

"Why did you enlist?" In every case the answer was the same. That memorable day in August came. Suddenly, the old haunts were desolate, the boon companions had gone. It was unthinkable to leave the danger to them and accept only the pleasures oneself, to go on enjoying the sweet things of life in defence of which they were perhaps even then shedding their blood in the north. Some day they would return, and with honor — not all, but some. The old order of things would have irrevocably vanished. There would be a new companionship whose bond would be the common danger run, the common sufferings borne, the common glory shared. "And where have you been all the time, and what have you been doing?" The very question would be a reproach, though none were intended. How could they endure it?

Seeger's "Letters" are as much to be read as his "Poems" for any adequate understanding of the wholly pagan and fatalistic philosophy which dominated this disciple of the absolute in beauty and freedom. In the first October of the war he was looking, like the rest of the world, for its early termination: "I think you can count on seeing me at Fairlea next summer, for I shall certainly return after the war to see you all and recuperate." Before the end of the year he was writing in his diary: "There will be war for many years to come in Europe and I shall continue to be a soldier as long as there is war." As the months wore on it became clearer still that a long war lay ahead, but from Seeger came only words of happiness that he was where he was, doing what he did. That was continually the hard work of a good soldier, living fully up to his belief that Strife played just as important a part in the world as Love.

> You must not be anxious [he wrote to his mother in June of 1915] about my not coming back. The chances are about ten to one that I will. But if I should not, you must be proud, like a Spartan mother, and feel that it is your contribution to the triumph of the cause whose righteousness you feel so keenly. Everybody should take part in this struggle which is to have so decisive an effect, not only on the nations engaged but on all humanity. There should be no neutrals but everyone should bear some part of the burden. If so large a part should fall to your share, you would be in so far superior to other women and should be correspondingly proud. There would be nothing to regret, for I could not have done otherwise than what I did and I think I could not have done better. Death is nothing terrible after all. It may mean something more wonderful than life. It cannot possibly mean anything worse to the good soldier. So do not be unhappy but no matter what happens walk with your head high and glory in your large share of whatever credit the world may give me.

The quotations from Seeger's "Letters and Diary" might be extended indefinitely. They would show him with his eyes unfalteringly fixed on the true objects of the conflict, enjoying the loveliness of nature and the pleasures of human intercourse — such as the meetings with his fellow Harvard graduates and *légionnaires*, Victor Chapman and Henry Farnsworth, — reading, thinking, leading in general the life out of which such poems as "Champagne (1914–15)," "I Have a Rendezvous with Death," and the "Ode in Memory of the American Volunteers Fallen for France" could naturally proceed. In the matter of outward circumstances, he will be found in the front-line trenches of Champagne before the end of October, 1914, on the Aisne, in Alsace, in the 1915–16 Battle of Champagne, sometimes *en repos* back of the lines, more often at the very front, slightly wounded in February, 1915, and, much later, invalided, through bronchitis, back to Biarritz, whence he wrote to his mother in March of 1916:

> I hope you got my letters from the hospital soon enough to be reassured about my not being at Verdun. Of course, to me it is a matter of great regret and I take it as a piece of hard luck. . . . All climates are alike to me, but the best now are those that smell of powder in the day and are lit by the *fusées éclairantes* at night.

Back at the Somme front he wrote significantly, to his *marraine* on June 1, 1916:

> The noticeable young man you describe as having seen at Lavenue's was probably myself, for it was my pleasure in those days to be noticeable just as now it is exactly the opposite. Where once it was my object to be individual, it is now an even greater satisfaction to merge into the whole, and feeling myself the smallest cog in the mighty machinery that is grinding out the future of the world, whatever that is to be.

These words were written immediately after Seeger's entirely human disappointment at being so much a cog in the machine that he failed to receive his *permission* to go to Paris and read in public his "Ode in Memory of the American Volunteers Fallen for France" — one of the small number of really beautiful poems brought forth by the war. Another poem, his last, a sonnet in which he looked beyond the days of war, was enclosed in a letter to his *marraine* written June 21, 1916, the day before his twenty-eighth birthday. He had been looking forward eagerly to participation in a great attack, and continued so to do. There was not long to wait. For several days he and his comrades were on the tiptoe of expectation. Seeger's friend and fellow *légionnaire*, Rif Baer, an Egyptian, has described the final scenes. This was the last of all:

> About four o'clock the order came to get ready for the attack. None could help thinking of what the next few hours would bring. One minute's anguish and then, once in the ranks, faces became calm and serene, a kind of gravity falling upon them, while on each could be read the determination and expectation of victory. Two battalions were to attack Belloy-en-Santerre, our company being the reserve of battalion. The companies forming the first wave were deployed on the plain. Bayonets glittered in the air above the corn, already quite tall.
>
> The first section (Alan's section) formed the right and vanguard of the company and mine formed the left wing. After the first bound forward, we lay flat on the ground, and I saw the first section advancing beyond us and making toward the extreme right of the village of Belloy-en-Santerre. I caught sight of Seeger and called to him, making a sign with my hand.
>
> He answered with a smile. How pale he was! His tall silhouette stood out on the green of the cornfield. He was the tallest man in his section. His head erect, and pride in his eye, I saw him running forward, with bayonet fixed. Soon he disappeared and that was the last time I saw my friend.

The village of Belloy-en-Santerre was taken, though Seeger, fallen, July 4, 1916, among the first in the attack, could but cheer his comrades on as they dashed past the spot where he lay dying. The fourth strophe of the Memorial Day Ode which he did not read in Paris should be read when he and other American volunteers of the earlier days of the war are remembered:

O friends! I know not since that war began
From which no people nobly stands aloof
If in all moments we have given proof
Of virtues that were thought American.
I know not if in all things done and said
All has been well and good,
Or if each one of us can hold his head
As proudly as he should,
Or, from the pattern of those mighty dead
Whose shades our country venerates today,
If we've not somewhat fallen and somewhat gone astray.
But you to whom our land's good name is dear,
If there be any here
Who wonder if her manhood be decreased,
Relaxed its sinews and its blood less red
Than that at Shiloh and Antietam shed,
Be proud of these, have joy in this at least,
And cry: "Now heaven be praised
That in that hour that most imperilled her,
Menaced her liberty who foremost raised
Europe's bright flag of freedom, some there were
Who, not unmindful of the antique debt,
Came back the generous path of Lafayette;
And when of a most formidable foe
She checked each onset, arduous to stem —
Foiled and frustrated them —
On those red fields where blow with furious blow
Was countered, whether the gigantic fray
Rolled by the Meuse or at the Bois Sabot,
Accents of ours were in the fierce mêlée;

And on those furthest rims of hallowed ground
Where the forlorn, the gallant charge expires,
When the slain bugler has long ceased to sound,
And on the tangled wires
The last wild rally staggers, crumbles, stops,
Withered beneath the shrapnel's iron showers: —
Now heaven be thanked, we gave a few brave drops;
Now heaven be thanked, a few brave drops were ours.

HENRY AUGUSTUS COIT

Class of 1910

Henry Augustus Coit, born at Concord, New Hampshire, May 26, 1888, was the only child of Joseph Howland Coit, president of the New York publishing house of Moffat, Yard and Company, and Adeline (Balch) Coit. His father's father was the Rev. Henry A. Coit, first rector of St. Paul's School, Concord; his mother's father was the Rev. Canon Lewis Balch, once rector of St. Bartholomew's Church, New York City, and for many years Secretary of the House of Bishops of the Protestant Episcopal Church.

The boy received his preparation for Harvard College at St. Paul's, and in the autumn of 1906 entered college with the Class of 1910. He remained at Harvard only two years. In the first of these he was captain of the freshman crew, having brought with him from Concord the interest and skill in rowing which St. Paul's has done so much to develop.

In the seven years between leaving college in 1908 and joining the British Army in Canada, Henry Coit was employed in New York State and Pennsylvania, by the Long Island Railroad Company and the Good Roads Machinery Company, and on a ranch in Klickitat County, Washington. In his turning from these pursuits to that of a soldier in the fight against Germany a succinct explanation is to be found in a letter to his mother from the "sister in charge" at the hospital in which he died: "I asked him once," wrote this Canadian nurse, "how it happened he was out fighting with us, coming from U.S.A." "Our fight, too," was his answer.

His military record is brief. On December 15, 1915, he enlisted at Montreal as a private in the Fifth University Overseas Company of Princess Patricia's Canadian Light Infantry — the only American in his company. From this date until March 15, 1916, he was in training at Montreal. On March 30 he sailed for England on the *Olympic*, convoyed by British warships, with his company and five thousand other Canadian troops and eighty nurses. From April 10 to June 1 he was in training for the front at Shorncliffe

— East and West Sandling. From East Sandling he wrote home on May 27: "Today six of us pottered about digging up little bits of grass around the officers' quarters, and we varied the programme somewhat, by killing sixteen rats, but when one is longing to get to France, grass pulling, rat killing, and baseball are hardly satisfactory." Again on May 31 he wrote: "The officers we have met here are splendid fellows, most of them. It is my luck to be asked when I am going to get a commission — but if you could see some of the young stiffs that have commissions, you would be tickled to death that I hadn't one, and I feel if I get recommended for a commission at the front, that's well and good — but I don't want it on pull. I think I would regret any step that separated me from my company, anyway, and it is one of the things I look forward to, fighting side by side with some of my pals to help put the Germans where they belong. And I won't put on paper where they should be.

"I am longing to go to France, and I'll do my bit the best I can."

From June 5 to July 3 he served in the trenches at the front, except for days in billet back of the line. On July 2 he was struck by a motor lorry near Ypres, and "dangerously wounded" through compound fractures of both knees. On July 5 he was taken to the Third Canadian Clearing Station at Remy Siding near Poperinghe. Here, after intense suffering, his right leg was amputated on August 4, the earliest time at which the surgeons believed him strong enough to stand the operation. Here, on August 7, his left leg was also amputated, and at nine o'clock that night he died.

When his parents in America heard of his injuries, they sailed at once for Europe, hoping to help him in person. In London they received bulletins of his condition, especially from a Church of England chaplain who was constantly seeing their son in the hospital. On August 3 he telegraphed himself to his father a message of affection and pleasure that they were so near him. In London they received the news of his death. Since then they have printed a small volume containing a number of letters from the chaplain and others who ministered to Henry Coit in the last month of his life. If it was denied him to show his qualities in battle with the enemy, they were memorably displayed in his fight with suffering. This is what the "sister in charge" wrote, in part, about him:

I want to tell you that among the wonderful, brave men that came to us here, your son stands almost preëminent. And every one that came in contact with him says the same thing.

He ever had a ready smile and answer, and even at the worst moments never lost his courage or courtesy for a second. Only a few days ago, he said to me, "You will have to lunch or dine with me when we get back to New York, sister" (though a Canadian, my nursing life was in New York City), "if you don't mind going somewhere with an old cripple."

So often, when he was having a hard time, I have said I was sorry, or it was too bad, or some such thing, and he would answer with his winning smile, "Never mind, sister, it is all in the old game!"

Never once did I hear him utter a complaint or regret. And we all loved the way, when we got him fruit or such, how he always wanted to share it with the others. So many who passed through the ward when he was there have written to ask about him, and so many P. P. C. L. I.'s have called to inquire about him.

Another bit of testimony is found in an "Extract from a letter from one of the staff attached to the Casualty Clearing Station":

The boy, Coit, whom you mention was here with us for more than four weeks — from the time he was wounded. Every day I saw and spoke to him. He was the gamest lad I have ever seen in all my experience with boys. He was a standing rebuke to those silly persons who suggest that Americans are lacking in courage. Sisters, surgeons, all of us loved that lad. In spite of suffering he always smiled. There was never a complaint or grumble from his lips. . . . That lad had blood and breeding. I have never seen such another case of heroism as his.

One night they thought he was dying, and I went into the ward where he was. Screens had been put about his bed. The chaplain sat by his side, holding his hand and repeating prayers. The nursing sister, who had been at the front from the first, was bathing his forehead, and weeping like a child. When the prayers ceased, Coit spoke about arrangements for his funeral. He was calmly heroic. He did not go then, but about two weeks later. . .

Young Coit's parents have every reason to be proud of such a son. For the last three weeks of his life it was his soul that kept his body going. He had absolutely no fear of death.

Yes, Coit was the bravest lad I have ever known.

"He never regretted his coming over here," his friend the chaplain wrote, "in spite of the accident which resulted"; and for the future — "he was ready to face it." His body was buried in the nearby cemetery on the Poperinghe Boeschepe road.

ROBERT EDOUARD PELLISSIER

Class of 1904

Robert Pellissier was both a native and a citizen of France. Having left France for America with his mother before he was fourteen, and having returned to his country but twice as a visitor, he was exempt by law from military service; but the same spirit which had held him from changing his French for American citizenship led him, immediately upon the coming of war, to sail for France and offer himself to its army. Just before sailing, in August of 1914, he wrote in a letter: "I don't know what use the Republic can make of me, but 'all men are needed' is the constant cry, and so, by Jove, I see no way out which does not mean the giving up of the prerogatives and privileges which go with the name man synonymous with gentleman."

His love of France was deeply rooted in his nature. He was born, May 12, 1882, at La Ferrière-sous-Jougne, Doubs, in the Jura Mountains. "The severe and almost tragic beauty of the fir-tree forests, extending for miles over the mountain-sides" — one of his sisters has written — "was so strongly stamped on his memory that he always longed for fir-clad mountains and loved those landscapes best which came nearest to this type of natural beauty." His parents were Marcel and Emma (Testuz) Pellissier — of substantial stock, with manufacturers, lawyers, and the critic, Georges Pellissier, on the father's side, and Protestant ministers, army officers, and a botanist of note, on the mother's. The father, Marcel Pellissier, superintendent of a wire and nail factory at La Ferrière, was himself an ardent patriot, devoted to the Huguenot traditions of his family. He died when Robert, the youngest of seven children, was only six years old, but the boy soon took to questioning the older brothers and sisters about their father and his teachings. What he learned is suggested by these words of his sister's concerning their life at La Ferrière:

> In this Roman Catholic community our family was the only one which was of Huguenot ancestry, and as the only Protestant church was several miles distant, our father, in his own way, gave us religious training. In summer, on Sunday, when the weather was fair, he often took us to a part of the forest where old fir-trees, standing wide apart, left an open space as dark and mysterious as a cathedral, and there he would read to us either a psalm of David or a passage from the Gospels, and the reading over, he would tell us how, in olden times, our Huguenot ancestors had fought for their faith and how for centuries before the great French Revolution, they had prayed and worshipped in

the wilderness, in some clearing or by the side of a stream. . . . The whole trend of this religious instruction was that external ceremonies are of but little importance and that the spiritual side of worship is the main thing.

The son's inheritance of the father's love for France revealed itself in a manner peculiarly French while Robert Pellissier was still a boy. After his father's death he went with his mother to Geneva, where they lived, and he went to school, for a few years. The suburb in which they made their home was very near the French border, and it is told that "he never spent a day without at least putting his foot on French soil." Such a Frenchman, grown to manhood, could not help returning to fight for *la patrie*.

All the intervening years, except for travel, were spent in America. He passed his fourteenth birthday, in 1896, on a steamer of the French Line bearing him and his mother to share the family life, in Brooklyn, of one of his sisters who was married. After three years in the Brooklyn public schools, for which he prepared himself in English during the summer holidays by translating "A Tale of Two Cities" both literally and idiomatically into French, he entered the Bridgewater (Massachusetts) State Normal School. A four years' course of study there (1899–1903) enabled him to enter the Senior Class of the Lawrence Scientific School at Harvard, on a Normal School Scholarship, in the autumn of 1903. When he and an Irish friend who had come with him from Bridgewater to Cambridge first looked at the Harvard Commencement Day programme in the following June they were dismayed at not finding their names at once among the recipients of degrees — but only, as they soon learned with infinite relief, because they appeared on a later page of the pamphlet among those to whom Honors had been awarded.

Looking upon the work which had won him his S.B. degree as preparatory to the study of medicine, Pellissier became a teacher of French, and incidentally of biology, at Williston Academy, Easthampton, Massachusetts, in order to earn the requisite funds. After a year of teaching a threat of tuberculosis showed him not only that his strength was inadequate to the arduous studies for the medical profession but that he must devote a year to establishing his health for advanced work of a less exacting nature, in Romance Languages. This he did with complete success, partly in France, partly in Western Massachusetts, and in a manner which caused a Williston colleague to write after his death: "The fight he made against insidious tuberculosis was heroic. It was an earnest of the valor which for two resolute years just closed he manifested on the Western front in France."

In 1908 he resigned his position at Williston and entered the Graduate School of Arts and Sciences at Harvard as a student of Romance Languages. On winning his A.M. degree in 1909, he went to Leland Stanford Jr. University for a year under a fellowship as a graduate student, serving at the same time as instructor in Romanic Languages. At the end of that academic year he came back to Cambridge, *via* the west coast, Mexico, and New Orleans, and reëntered the Graduate School. In 1913 he received the degree of Ph.D. His thesis, "The Neo-Classic Movement in Spain during the Eighteenth Century," has since been published by Leland Stanford Jr. University, with an introduction by Professor Grandgent. His letters from the front show that this was not his last piece of scholarly production. On July 19, 1915, he wrote: "Did you see my book? The Oxford Press, American Branch, New York, sent me a copy of it. My sister did all the proof-reading, so there are no mistakes in spelling. Thanks to her and to me the Great American Public has now a School Edition of Racine's *Bérénice*. I may make five dollars on it, this coming academic year; nothing like the prospect of great wealth to make life rosy."

After a pleasure trip through France and Spain in the summer of 1913, Pellissier entered again upon the teaching of Romance Languages at Leland Stanford Jr., and had performed this work for a year and received his appointment as Assistant Professor when the war came. The spirit in which he took the responsibilities it imposed upon him has already been indicated. On leave of absence from the University, extended to cover the brief remainder of his life, he offered himself for military service in France just as soon as the long journey from California would permit. Two months of military drill at Besançon, in his native department of Doubs, placed him in the Fifth Battalion of the *chasseurs à pied* — an élite branch of the French Army, distinguished from the line infantry, the *pitous*, who were expected to march about eighteen miles a day, by a corresponding expectation, as he once expressed it, "to go as much as thirty with the whole load." Though not trained, like the *chasseurs alpins*, primarily for mountain service, the regiment of "Blue Devils" to which Pellissier belonged was ordered at once to the Vosges, a region in which his early delight in the novels of Erckmann-Chatrian gave him a special interest. Here he took part in trench warfare of the most exacting nature until, at the end of January, 1915, near Steinbach, he was wounded in the shoulder. Though his wound was healed after four months in hospital, the condition of his shoulder would not permit him to carry a knapsack. Accordingly, he determined to prepare himself for a commission, passed the examinations for the officers' training school at Saint-Maixent, where he spent four months of study, returning to the front before the end of 1915 with the grade of sergeant, but so well prepared for the commission he was soon to receive that in the absences of a lieutenant he acted for weeks at a time in his place. His first service, after his long absence from the front was again in Alsace and in the neighborhood of Verdun during the most savage fighting of the early months of 1916. His battalion left the mountains before the end of June, and before the end of August was helping to fight the Battle of the Somme, and was in constant action in the neighborhood of Péronne. Here, on August 29, Pellissier was killed at Cléry. On August 27 he had written a friend as follows:

It seems that we are going to attack and I do not wish to take part in this affair without writing a few words to you. It is perfectly possible that I may come out unscathed, like many others, but it is also possible that I may not. I am writing to my brother John, a letter of general interest. If I should not come back, you would tell him, that to the last my thoughts were with him and with our family in America and also that I do not regret the choice I made in returning to France. This will seem very foolish if tomorrow or the day after I should return as usual, but you will certainly understand that at this time I cannot refrain from looking at all the possibilities and be silent.

It was not "tomorrow," but early in the morning of "the day after" that he received the wound from which he died before night. His battalion had been relieved, and to him was assigned the task, usually an officer's, of remaining in the sector when all his comrades had left and giving the countersign to those who were to take their places. While thus alone he was shot through the chest by the ball of a *mitrailleuse*, fulfilling his duty in a post of trust.

This brave soldier was primarily an intellectual, and a humanist. The volume of "Letters from a Chasseur à Pied: Robert Pellissier," printed for his sister, Miss Adeline Pellissier in 1917, reveals him clearly in this light. It contains many passages describing life in the French Army as many other soldiers saw it. It discloses also the individual point of view of a thoughtful, cultivated man, and the few quotations from it for which a place may here be found are chosen with this end in view:

September 14, 1914.

Several hundred thousand men have just been killed or are exposed to imminent death. Yet the thousands who remain are calm and follow their daily routine. I understand why a great patriotic drama is hardly ever immortalized through an artistic interpretation at the time it took place. Did the poets of the fifteenth century have any inkling of what Joan of Arc was to mean to posterity? Perspective is lacking. It is only later, much later, that people come to realize that the fate of a nation depended upon a certain event.

October 12, 1914.

Everything would be satisfactory were it not that yesterday while taking a leap, the last one in the drill, I hurt my knee, bruising it badly; now it is swollen. The medical examiner having sent me to the infirmary, I witnessed the cleaning of a wound. I had to leave the ward and on reaching the corridor I fainted, falling on the floor full length. The worst of it is that this accident has taken away my self-confidence — my knee, the rain, the straw, the remembrance of my mishap, — all these things depress me more than I can tell. What shall I do in the trenches?

Christmas, 1914.

Men become religious in war time. On Christmas day our officers went to mass in state and style. Yesterday I had some fun watching various kinds of *chasseurs* and dragoons and muleteers and artillery men sneaking into the church, coming by the back way and progressing cautiously and somewhat sheepishly towards the church, opening the door stealthily and entering crab fashion. Bold bad boys in ordinary times and weather, but made meek by the events.

January 14, 1915.

I am glad you heard Brieux. I have read about ten of his plays. I always liked him because of his virility. He stands in fine contrast with a good many of our modern writers who are altogether too supple. From a moral standpoint I hate flabbiness. I am more of a Huguenot than most people think.

January 28, 1915.

The French are a pretty brave race, believe me, and the only real darn fools in the lot are those who write novels about them. If I ever get back to Stanford I shall give a course on the French novel with a view to rehabilitating the race. I am putting all manner of curious and interesting facts in my diary, which one hundred years from now should be worth millions of dollars from an historical standpoint.

February 7, 1915.

Since I have been here the Germans attacked twice, and got theirs richly each time. The first time was on the Kaiser's birthday and they came up by fours, shouting drunk and got cleaned out. The second time they came in hordes, rushed two trenches and pinched a rapid fire gun, whereupon our commander came along, drew his revolver and my friends charged with him, kicked the Dutch out of the trenches, got hold of the machine gun and made a lot of prisoners. I have been told that the ground in front of the trenches is gray with German uniforms. One of our captains wept when he saw the slaughter of Germans, for young men are young men, even when they are Germans. These slaughters take place at dusk or at night. Such is war, Tim!

February 11, 1915.

For a decadent race, the French are doing well; but good Heavens, what a futile and a criminal thing war is. No one who has not seen it can realize how wicked it is. Only an ass or a bandit can talk about the necessity or the beauty of war.

(*March, 1915.*)

Anatole France, Bourget, and Barrès are men of morbid temperament. In support of their weakness they place all the resources of a skillful dialectic which used in favor of a good cause might do much good and people come to think that it is freedom of thought which has created such a temperament while as a matter of fact it is their temperament which has given a twist to their minds. . . . I always felt that these writers were in no way the leaders of French thought. From a moral viewpoint, they are the wretched descendants, the last heirs of a long line of fast *esthètes,* which have for a common ancestor Chateaubriand, as he appears in the *Génie du Christianisme.* These people cannot teach anything to the young men of modern France. As leaders of the new generation, they have made a dismal failure. Barrès especially, who at one time had high pretensions in this respect. Young men turned to other writers like R. Rolland and Brieux, who were not obliged to display so much art in defense of temperamental weakness.

April 22, 1915.

The one decent thing that may come out of this horrible mess may be the final discrediting of war in Europe, and perhaps elsewhere. It's an idea which keeps up French soldiers at present.

One often hears them say, "Well, whatever happens to us, our children at least will be freed from the curse of militarism and all allied curses!"

September 12, 1915.

No, don't believe what Miss Addams is telling or rather what she has been told. French soldiers don't get drunk each time they go into a bayonet charge. I took part in one, and not only we had nothing in our cans except water, but we had had nothing to eat since breakfast (and it was two in the afternoon), and we had no supper at all and breakfast only at ten the next morning. I saw a charge start right from the very part of the trench where I sat and what struck me was the perfectly cold determination of the men who were to my left and to my right and in front of me. Those who cut lanes through our wires hit rhythmically and with perfect aim. There was no bar-room atmosphere at all. The men in the school here come from all corners and quarters of the front. I have asked a dozen or so of those who have charged with the bayonet what they knew about systematical distribution of whiskey or what not and they told me that they knew nothing about it, had always gone to it in the full possession of their powers.

October 24, 1915.

If I come through this war, I shall fight for the United States in all their wars to come in my life time.

November 7, 1915.

I'll tell you in secret that the army is made up largely of men who are hoping and piously praying that something ridiculous may happen to their betters.

November 21, 1915.

I don't believe that your country would lose very much by having something of an armed force. The rich must be strong, they must be willing to sacrifice something to remain rich. If France were a poor country, the hungry Germans who have grown too fast for their own good and for that of their neighbors, would not be bothering us from Dunkerque to Gallipoli. I don't believe that armies bring about war. If a man has a dollar he puts it in his pocket, if he has several hundred he puts them in a reënforced concrete, iron-clad, steel-rimmed, double-bottom bank and burglars immediately surround the bank and get busy with dynamite and all kinds of jimmies.

(*January, 1916.*)

If I pull out of this long drawn out scrape, I shall have gained one inestimable thing, absolute faith in the soundness of our race. How utterly ridiculous the decadence yarn seems, in the face of facts, of deeds. When the Germans attack us they are often drunk as drunk can be; they howl and shriek; they come in hordes. Our men go at it in the full control of their faculties and without the imperious need of feeling the comforting touch of the elbows of neighbors.

March 6, 1916.

No, I do not hate wholesale fashion. I even believe that I do not hate at all in the literal sense of the word. If on a fine night when crossing the campus on my way back from Palo Alto, I should encounter a hold-up man, thrusting his revolver at me, I should do my best to smash his face, but once the deed was accomplished, I should be perfectly willing to have him taken at my expense to the Peninsula Hospital. It is the kind of feeling I have when fighting the Boches. Against the Boches taken singly, I have no grudge, but I am perfectly determined not to allow my linguistic and idealistic family group to be swallowed up by theirs, which at the present time is certainly far from showing moral superiority. Have you read "Above the Strife," by Romain Rolland? I have not, but the title appeals to me and the author has been attacked so unanimously by the most sensational newspapers that I dare say he must have voiced some kind of truth in a vigorous manner. The Boches, however, are disconcerting to a degree when it comes to knavery and fanaticism. Well, what I ask of you is not to consider me a blind monster, for it is not with joy that I put my finger on the trigger but I go through with that motion, whether I like it or not, and I shall continue to do so. It is a disgusting job, but it has to be done — so help me God! — if in so doing I incur everlasting condemnation.

August 6, 1916.

In spite of the *Lusitania,* Wilson may loom big yet in the history of the world. I absolutely refuse to put a small dingy political motive back of his foreign policy. It seems to me that he acted logically as representing a nation made up largely of convinced pacifists. It is not time to talk peace now in France, but after the war it will be a shame if all the fine and generous movements for general peace which were at the bottom of most political discussions are not taken up again and with more vigor. After two years of this fighting business I can't agree with those who say that there will always be war, and any man who has the generosity to fight for peace *envers et contre tous* seems to me most respectable. It's very easy for a Roosevelt to be popular. All one needs to do is to appeal to the cowardice of those who are afraid and to the passions of those who are, above all, proud or vain or greedy. Wilson could have been immensely popular with California, New Mexico, Arizona, Colorado and a good part of the Mississippi Valley simply by getting hold of a few Mexican border states, giving poor downtrodden promoters a chance to get fatter.

Romain Rolland is getting damned up and down because he keeps airing his belief that in spite of all things done, there may yet be a few good Germans in the world. He is very much more creditable to his nation than that ass of Saint-Saëns, who since the Belgian and Northern atrocities, has discovered that Wagner had no musical sense at all. It would be too bad for France if there were a dozen Romain Rollands writing and talking, but it would be a sign of mortal disease in the nation if all thinkers and all professional men were of the Saint-Saëns stripe. A confirmed unabashed, untractable idealist here and there is a beacon light, no matter how destructive his theories would be if applied without discrimination. It seems to me that Wilson is a Puritanical idealist whose mistakes will be more than made up for by the new orientation which foreign affairs in the United States may get from his principles of patience and forbearance. What made me write out this "tartine" is the fact that I have often to explain the United States to the men here who, being ill informed and not analytical, think that the United States were afraid to fight Germany! As foolish an opinion of you as so many of your *bourgeois* had of us *ante bellum.*

It remains to be said that the *Journal Officiel* of October 14, 1916, recorded in the following terms the award of the *Médaille Militaire*, together with the *Croix de Guerre avec palme* to

"Robert Edouard Pellissier,

M[le] 04682, sergent à la 1re compagnie du 5me bataillon de chasseurs à pied: Sous-officier d'une bravoure et d'un sang-froid remarquables. La section ayant été soumise pendant plusieurs jours à un violent bombardement, n'a cessé d'exalter le moral de ses hommes et de porter secours aux blessés. A été atteint d'une très grave blessure lors d'une relève particulièrement difficile."

Two ambulances sent to the front commemorated the affection in which he was held by American friends: one from Bridgewater State Normal School, another from Leland Stanford Jr. University. At Stanford the mere announcement that contributions would be received was enough to secure the requisite fund, to which nobody was asked to contribute.

JOHN CUTHBERT STAIRS

LAW 1913–14

JOHN CUTHBERT STAIRS was born at Halifax, Nova Scotia, December 3, 1892, a son of George and Helen Elizabeth (Mackenzie) Stairs, and graduated at Dalhousie College in 1912. While an undergraduate he played on the Dalhousie football team. In Halifax he is remembered as a young man of strong personal charm, who made many friends and always held them. He attended the Harvard Law School for one year only. When the war broke out he was in Calgary, where he expected to gain a summer's experience in the law office of a friend, but returned at once to Halifax to report to his militia regiment, the 66th Princess Louise Fusileers, and volunteered in August, 1914, for overseas service. After serving as lieutenant at a harbor post near Halifax from August to November, he received orders to report to the 25th Nova Scotia Battalion, just formed for service overseas, and in May, 1915, sailed for England as a lieutenant in this battalion. His training in England lasted through the summer; in September he went to France with his regiment.

In the fighting at Ypres he took an immediate part, and in October was so severely wounded in the leg that he was obliged to return to England for convalescence. In March, 1916, he went back to France, where he saw fighting at St. Éloi and was mentioned in despatches. Then his old battalion, the 25th, was marched to the Somme. In the action of September 15, in which the battalion captured the village of Courcelotte, and won for itself many honors, Stairs, now holding the rank of captain, was killed. He was buried behind the lines in a Canadian cemetery at Albert.

On the same day a brother of Captain Stairs, fighting also at Courcelotte, won the Military Cross. Another brother had been killed at Ypres, April 24, 1915. Five first cousins of these young men gave their lives in the war. Such has been the toll of Canada.

DILLWYN PARRISH STARR

Class of 1908

Dill Starr, as he was known in that public familiarity which attaches to conspicuous players of college football, came to Harvard from Groton School in the autumn of 1904. At Groton he had been captain of the School eleven. "I remember Dill with much affection during his Groton days," wrote the Rector of the School soon after his former pupil's death. "He was 'all boy' then. Simple and straightforward and afraid of nothing. I fancy he kept these boyish qualities to the end." So indeed he appears to have done, for "The War Story of Dillwyn Parrish Starr," printed by his father in 1917 for private distribution, reveals a young soldier to whom the terms that fitted the boy may most aptly be applied.

They fitted him also during his four years in college as a member of the Class of 1908. He was still "all boy"— to the extent of not taking his studies seriously enough to win him his bachelor's degree. In the social and athletic pursuits of undergraduates his personal charm and his prowess carried him far. He was a member of the Institute of 1770, the Kalumet, Round Table, Hasty Pudding, and Porcellian Clubs. But it was as a football player that he really made his name in College. In each of his four college years he was a member of the University eleven, as quarter-back when a freshman and a sophomore, as right end when a junior, and left end in his senior year — "all boy" and "afraid of nothing." A reminiscence of his college days carries with it a suggestion of the spirit which animated his playing of football, and at the same time foreshadows, as if in prophecy, the end that awaited him. When it came a classmate wrote: "There is one comforting thought and that is that I am sure he died as he would wish to die. On the wall of the breakfast-room at the Club at Cambridge there is a picture of a cavalry charge with an officer, with sword upraised, leading his men on gallantly. Dill and I would often get seats at dinner opposite this picture; would discuss the splendid sensations such a man must have under the circumstances, and we would always agree that if we might choose the kind of death we would have, we should choose such an ending."

Starr's home was in Philadelphia, where he was born October 3, 1884, the son of Dr. Louis Starr, a widely known specialist in children's diseases, long a professor in the Medical School of the University of Pennsylvania, and Mary (Parrish) Starr. Both English and French blood were transmitted to him from earlier generations, and the Quaker inheritances which belong to many true Pennsylvanians. After leaving college Starr was employed in business offices in Philadelphia and New York. At the outbreak of the war he was passing his summer holiday with his family at Islesboro, Maine. Late in August he went to New York, where foreign affairs seemed less remote, and "on Labor Day," to quote the words of his father, "while lying on the sands at Long Beach reading the war reports, he suddenly told the friends who were with him that he had determined 'to see the war.'"

The opportunity so to do was speedily sought and found. On September 13, 1914, he sailed from New York as one of the crew of the Red Cross ship *Hamburg*, carrying medical supplies and a corps of surgeons and nurses to France. The eleventh-hour substitution of an untrained crew for the Germans who had previously manned the vessel made the voyage both uncomfortable and perilous. But Starr made friends with the chief engineer, and, bearing a signed certificate of ability and character from him, was permitted to leave the ship at Falmouth. Thence he went direct to London where, within a few days, he met Richard Norton, then establishing his "American Volunteer Motor Ambulance Corps," and offered himself for the service of this organization. The offer was accepted, and, after a short period of special training for the work of the Corps and securing his outfit, he left London for the front, October 19.

Starr's connection with Richard Norton's motor corps lasted only about two months. In that time he did good work as an ambulance driver, and had his eyes fully opened to the realities of the war for those who were fighting it. "I know that from the very first," his father has written, "he disliked the idea of being protected by a red cross on his sleeve, while so many about him were enlisted to do soldiers' work." It is not surprising, therefore, that when the opportunity came to him early in December to enter a more active service he seized it, and enlisted, with his friend Walter G. Oakman, Jr., of the Harvard Class of 1907, in the British Armoured Motor Car Division, a branch — one does not see just why — of the Royal Naval Air Service. It was at this point in his war record that his father says "the conviction grew strong within him that the place for a free man was on the side of the Allies fighting for liberty, justice, civilization — the world's cause; and he began to feel, too, the importance of the issue to his own country."

From early in December until March 1, 1915, Starr was under constant training in England for the work of the Armoured Motor Corps Division. On March 1 he left London for the front, in a squadron commanded by the Duke of Westminster, and made up of twelve light and three heavy cars, several supply cars, and twenty-four motor-cycles for dispatch work. There were eight officers and one hundred and twenty men. Each car had a name of its own, and Starr's was called the "Black Joke." They sailed from Dover, March 6, and disembarked at Dunkirk the next day.

Again Starr was to have about two months of continuous service in France. In the course of it he took part in a number of actions, including the Battle of Neuve Chapelle. There were alternations of perilous service and fatigue duty. Of the first he wrote one day in his diary: "Thinking of going in gives one the same feeling as before a football match." It may well have been during his performance of fatigue duty that he recorded his unflattering opinion of one of his fellows with whom he had disagreed, and followed it up by an entry which his father has preserved as illustrating his sweetness of disposition: "I suppose I'm a chump for writing this but it relieves my mind." After a few days he added: "Here and now I take back all I said of ——. I have been with him under fire and he was cool as a cucumber. But I will leave it in just to show what a goat I am."

He had not been making any such impression upon his superior, for on May 10 the Duke of Westminster told Starr, and Oakman, that they had been promoted, and were to report in London. This they did, a week later, and in another ten days Starr was gazetted sub-lieutenant, Royal Navy Volunteer Reserves, corresponding in rank with that of full lieutenant in the army. At this time he received an offer for duty in Gallipoli, where two Armoured Car Squadrons had already gone, and accepted it with enthusiasm for the prospect of active service which it afforded. On June 7 he sailed to join the ill-fated expedition to the Dardanelles, the only man on the Harvard Roll of Honor who bore a part in this tragic experience.

Starr had about four active months of it. He did not reach Gallipoli till after the middle of July, and left it November 13. His letters written in this period confirm the general impression of the grimness and horror of the situation at the Dardanelles. He saw hard fighting in and out of the trenches — and such sights as this glimpse recorded after three weeks on the Peninsula suggests: "A man went mad on the beach today, and began shooting about, and they had to kill him. It's a cheerful life, isn't it?" A little later he wrote: "I am constantly in hot water about home as all here know I am an American, and the notes about the *Lusitania* aren't making us any too popular. Although my commander is friendly, I sometimes get furious." Nor were the conditions of his service wholly agreeable. "We hear again," he wrote on September 9, "that the Armoured Cars are going to be disbanded. Word has come that there are no more reserves for us and that when our numbers are exhausted by sickness and wounds we are to turn our guns over to the army. You can see how discouraging it is, and I really don't think it worth our while sitting here all winter doing nothing. The Army doesn't recognize us because we belong to the R.N.A.S., neither does the Navy, because we are acting on land." Frequent swims in the delicious water reminding him of home, in spite of sharks, yielded some enjoyment, but discouragement and discontent with the management of military matters, both at home and at the front, gave the period their own sombre color. Evidently, Starr was again rendering a good account of himself; at the beginning of November he received an offer of transfer to an army brigade from the general commanding it, with a promise of a captaincy in the near future. But this would not have meant France, where Starr by this time was hoping to serve again. A few days later, incapacitated by dysentery, he was sent to a base hospital, and here on November 12 he received an Admiralty order to report in London. The next day he sailed for England, his question of further service on the Peninsula solved for him.

His family, awaiting him in London, found him changed. "He seemed to have dropped much of his youthfulness, and to have become more serious and possessed by a more purposeful energy. These changes showed in his manner and in the expression of his face, while his steadfast eyes looked as if they had seen many grave sights, and, as has been said of a recent picture of him, as if one could read in them the whole history of the war. He seemed not to care to talk much of Gallipoli, and in what he said there was little reference to the dangers he had passed through or to hardships endured." Yet of the effect of the whole ordeal upon Dillwyn Starr his father says further: "He came through it with unbroken nerve, a more thoughtful, serious man, and mentally and physically a better soldier."

Reporting at the Admiralty Starr learned that the Armoured Car Division was in process of disbanding. Several alternatives were presented to him, including honorable discharge. This, his father and he decided, was not to be considered while the Allies were in the straits then existing. After weighing the several opportunities within reach, Starr chose a commission of second lieutenant in the Coldstream Guards, which his friend Oakman had already joined. The discipline and tradition of this regiment were unsurpassed in the British Army. Starr's previous service was well enough, but as a Coldstream Guardsman he still had much to learn, and from January 5 to July 11, 1916, he remained in England. Then, with four other Coldstream officers, he went to the front.

For the remainder of July, for all of August and a portion of September, Starr's letters show him in the front line and reserve trenches, and back of the line. He writes of a swim in the Somme, and a game of football with the Grenadiers, in which, he says, "I was lucky enough to make a goal for our side in the last thirty seconds." It was soccer, of which he had written the day before, "I don't know the first thing about it"; but his colonel said afterwards, "He was the best football player I ever saw." These were the interludes. The names of Albert and other places synonymous with bitter fighting spot the pages of his letters. In the last of them, dated September 12, 1916, he wrote, "We are going up in the line tomorrow or next day, so if you don't hear from me for a few days, don't worry." The point in the line to be attacked by the Second Battalion of the Coldstream Guards was at Ginchy, where the Germans held a strong position, the breaking of which was a matter of serious moment. Starr was chosen to lead a company of two platoons, his own, Number 12, and another, because "his men were certain to follow him anywhere." The desire which he had felt as a collegian to lead a charge in battle had frequently recurred in the two years of wartime. At last the moment was come. The following passage from Dr. Starr's narrative depicts the scene and the brave death that ended his son's part in it:

It was understood that at 5.40 o'clock on the morning of the fifteenth a squadron of "Tanks" were to advance from the rear along the sunken road and silence the machine-guns there. At 6.20 the Guards were to "go over."

True to the appointed time the "Tanks" were heard to start and, under heavy gun-fire, to come on a little way. Then they stopped! Every man in the Coldstream trench realized the import of this failure. One of the non-commissioned officers spoke to Dillwyn about it and was answered "I know, but we will go on without them." From this time, piecing together the bits of the story as they have reached me, I can picture him as the fixed moment approached, full of eagerness and suppressed energy and without the slightest trace of fear, standing with one foot so placed in a niche in the trench that he could leap to the top and over at the instant time was up, and hear him say, "five minutes more, men," "one minute more, men," and "time's up." Then, they tell me, he sprang on to the parapet, revolver in hand, and waving his stick and shouting, "Come on, twelve platoon, come on," leapt over and led on the charge. They went out into a perfect storm of shells and a hail of machine-gun bullets, a direct fire from the short trench in front of them and an enfilading fire from the uncleared road to the left. But they pressed on, he always well in front of his rapidly thinning platoons. They reached the short trench and here Dillwyn fell, just as he was springing upon its parapet, with his face to the enemy, shot through the heart, and killed instantly. His men, after a severe struggle, took the trench and, with the wave of support, swept by him. Less resistance was offered at the second trench, and when they reached the main trench the few who were left occupied it without any difficulty, as the Germans were on the run, and held it securely until they were relieved next day to take part in the capture of Lesboeufs.

Thus, Dillwyn Starr died, September 15, 1916, in the Battle of the Somme. The charge of the Guards in which he fell — a charge conducted, as one observer saw it, "as steadily as though they were walking down the Mall" — was a splendid example of the spirit of this regiment, and filled all England with pride. Starr's part in it received the highest praise from his fellow-officers and his men. A lieutenant of the regiment — and to this rank, it should be said, Starr himself was promoted by seniority at the very time of his death — wrote of him a fortnight after the action: "Officers and men were equally fond of him, and they all felt that before he was an officer, before he was an American, before anything, he was a MAN, and a man whom they could trust."

His body lies where he fell in France. Soon after his death his fellow-members of the Porcellian Club undertook the maintenance of an endowed bed in the American Ambulance Hospital in Paris, and placed over it a brass tablet with the inscription:

SUPPORTED BY THE PORCELLIAN CLUB
IN MEMORY OF DILLWYN PARRISH STARR.

He and his comrades, officers and men, of the Coldstream Guards who fell in the Battle of the Somme were commemorated in a special service at Holy Trinity Church, Sloane Street, London, on October 5. A service in memory of Starr alone was held in Trinity Church, New York City, three days earlier. After this service the flowers sent by friends were laid on the graves in Trinity Churchyard, especially on those of soldiers in the American Revolution.

WILLIAM STOCKS LACEY

D.M.D. 1913

WILLIAM STOCKS LACEY was born in Hertford, England, April 4, 1887, the only son of William J. M. Lacey, a dental surgeon in Hertford, and Elizabeth Mary (Stocks) Lacey. He entered the Harvard Dental School in 1912, from Guy's Hospital, London, with the British appellations of L.R.C.P., London, M.R.C.S., England, and L.D.S., England. He received his degree of Doctor of Dental Medicine at Harvard in 1913. In October of that year he married in England the only daughter of Major and Mrs. Thomas Barber of Hertford.

His rank in the British Army, which he joined January 1, 1916, was that of lieutenant in the Royal Army Medical Corps. A member of the 140th Field Ambulance, he was temporarily attached to the 11th Battalion, Royal West Kent Regiment, at the time of his death. This occurred October 11, 1916, at the 38th Casualty Clearing Station, France, in consequence of wounds received in action on the Somme two days before.

His father has written as follows of his final deeds of courage and mercy: "My son was wounded whilst attending to wounded soldiers on the field, out in the open. From what we have been told it appears that a large number of men had been wounded but could not be brought in. It was necessary for someone to give immediate help to the sufferers. This duty was performed by my son. He rendered it possible for all the wounded to be removed to dressing stations, when he was struck by a fragment of a shell which penetrated the lower part of the abdomen. He walked two miles to a dressing station, where an operation was performed. 'Gas gangrene' supervened and a second operation was necessary, after which he lived but a few hours."

He is buried at Heilly Station Cemetery, Mericourt l'Abbé, France.

NORMAN PRINCE

Class of 1908

Norman Prince was born at Pride's Crossing, Massachusetts, August 31, 1887, the second of the two sons of Frederick Henry and Abigail (Norman) Prince. His name identified him with his two grandfathers, Frederick O. Prince, once Mayor of Boston, and George H. Norman, a well-known citizen of Newport, Rhode Island. A notable energy, both of mind and of body, was evident in him as a boy. When he was about eleven he needed a tutor in Latin, and undertook the task of securing one for himself. He wanted to find somebody who would pilot him through six books of Virgil in two weeks. Interviewing the man he thought capable of this feat, he asked him how fast he could translate Virgil, and on receiving an estimate of "ten lines a minute," inquired eagerly, as he pulled out a stop watch, "May I time you, Sir?" This he did, with results so satisfactory that he insisted on persuading the tutor, somewhat against his will, to give him lessons between seven and eight in the morning and nine and ten at night. Several years later, while he was a pupil at Groton School, the chance to spend what would normally have been his sixth form year at school in Europe with his brother suddenly presented itself, and with the consent of the Groton and Harvard authorities he offered himself for the college entrance examinations, which he passed, without conditions, at the age of fifteen. This enabled him to study both in Germany and at Oxford before entering Harvard when the Class of 1908, with which he took his degree of A.B., *cum laude*, was beginning its sophomore year. In 1911 he graduated from the Harvard Law School.

His physical energy found an early outlet on the hunting field. He began riding to the hounds at Myopia when he was only seven. Before he and his brother went to Groton, their father forbade them one day to go to the meet, as it was raining hard and the riding was dangerous. They disobeyed him, and, besides hunting, raced their ponies, which collided and threw the boys so violently that one broke his thigh, the other his collar-bone. The older brother regained consciousness first, and soon heard Norman, with the broken thigh, saying, "Fred, I think I am dead. How do you feel?"

To such a boy, grown somewhat older, aviation was bound to appeal. When he finished his law studies it was with difficulty that his family persuaded him to take up the practice of his profession, for he was already becoming a skilful aviator, and cared for nothing else so much as for flying. For some time, indeed, after studying this science with the Wright brothers in Ohio and Starling Burgess at Marblehead, he was flying at high altitudes under an assumed name, both to escape notoriety and to avoid contentions with his family over the object of his heart's desire.

In the summer of 1911 he entered the employ of the law firm of Winston, Payne, Strawn, and Shaw in Chicago, where he remained until the summer of 1913. Then, because of trouble with his eyes, he dropped his legal work, and passed the year before the war at his father's house in Massachusetts, and at Pau. He had been much in France before, and the outbreak of the fight found him ready to do whatever he could for a country he loved like his own.

Obviously the best way for him to help France was as an aviator. This he did, not only as an intrepid individual flyer, but as the prime mover in the organization of the Lafayette Escadrille of the French Army, that squadron of American aviators to whom fell the honor of carrying the American flag first of all into the fighting at the front. One of his most active colleagues in the formation of this unit, Frazier Curtis, of the Harvard Class of 1898, has written: "The first time the idea of an American Escadrille came to Norman was probably at Marblehead in November, 1914, when he suggested it to me as we were flying together." In the following month Prince sailed for France, and in January volunteered for service in the French Army — *jusqu'au bout.* He was sent to a military aviation school at Pau for training, and in February telegraphed to Curtis, who by that time was flying in England, asking him to come to Paris and help in forwarding the plans for an American Escadrille which he had proposed to the French War Office. Curtis immediately met him in Paris, and with Elliot C. Cowdin (Harvard, '09), and others joined in the endeavor to make a reality of Prince's cherished idea. The obstacles that had to be overcome, and the deferred accomplishment of the plan in its fullness were related by Cowdin in the *Harvard Alumni Bulletin* of March 7, 1918, with a hearty recognition of Prince's leadership in the enterprise. "To Norman Prince," Curtis has also written, " is due the credit for the idea of an American Escadrille and for its organization under very discouraging circumstances."

It would be superfluous to relate them in detail in this place. They illustrated the same energy and tenacity of purpose which made Prince the brilliant aviator he was. He was not a writer of letters describing his experiences and sensations in the air. But on one occasion, when he returned to America for a brief holiday at the Christmas season of 1915, he made a speech in the Tavern Club of Boston, at a dinner given in his honor, and fortunately his words were preserved. Some of them are quoted here from the commemorative volume, "Norman Prince, a Volunteer Who Died for the Cause He Loved, with a Memoir by George F. Babbitt" (Harvard, '72). The two passages that follow describe his first bombing expedition and a later experience:

I have a vivid remembrance of my first bombarding expedition. The action took place at a point not far within the enemy's lines. I was sent with two or three members of my squadron to bombard a station where ammunition was being unloaded. It takes about forty minutes for a machine heavily loaded with bombs to get to a sufficient height to cross the lines. The minimum height at which we crossed was about seven thousand feet. I saw my comrades cross ahead of me and noted they were being heavily shelled by the enemy. Accordingly, I decided to go a little higher before crossing. When I found I had only sufficient gasoline left to make my bombardment and return to my base, I started over. I was soon to experience what I may call my baptism of fire. The impression made upon me by the terrible racket and the spectacle of shells aimed at me and exploding near by made me shiver for a moment. Though I was confident and unafraid, my limbs began to tremble. Still I kept straight on my course. I would not have changed it for the world. My legs were so wobbly from nervous excitement that I tried to hide them from my observer, who was an old hand at the game. I confess to a feeling of relief when I reached the point where our bombs were to be thrown over. Having discharged this duty I was glad to return to my starting-point with the motor running at slow speed, and knowing that I was soon to be out of range of the enemy's deadly fire.

One day six German machines, fully equipped, bombarded Nancy and our aviation field. To retaliate, my squadron was sent out to bombard their field on the same afternoon. We started with thirty machines to a designated rendezvous and fifty minutes later, after getting grouped, we proceeded to our ultimate destination. I had a very fast machine, and reached the German flying field without being hit. When about to let go my bombs and while my observer was aiming at the hangars of the

Germans my machine was attacked by them — one on the left and two on the right. I shouted to my observer to drop his bombs, which he did, and we immediately straightened out for home. While I was on the bank the Germans opened fire on me with their machine-guns which were even more perilous than their shells. My motor stopped a few moments afterwards. It had given out and to make matters worse a fourth German machine came directly at us in front. My observer, who was an excellent shot, let go at him with the result that when last seen this German aeroplane was about four hundred feet below and quite beyond control. The other Germans behind kept bothering us. If they had possessed ordinary courage, they might have got us. Flying without any motive power compelled me to stand my machine on end to keep ahead of them. As we were nearing the French lines these Germans left us. As I was barely moving I made an excellent target. One shell burst near enough to put shrapnel in my machine. It is marvelous how hard we can be hit by shrapnel and have no vital part of our equipment injured. I knew I was now over the French lines, which I must have crossed at a height of about four hundred metres. I finally landed in a field covered with white crosses marking the graves of the French and German soldiers who had fallen the previous September at this point. This was the battle the Kaiser himself came to witness, expecting to spend that night in Nancy.

If Mr. George Sylvester Viereck could have had his way during the visit to America in the course of which the speech in Boston was made, Prince would not have returned so promptly to France; but the efforts of the editor of *The Fatherland* to prevent the aviator, through action on the part of our government, from rejoining the French Army were unavailing, and at the very beginning of 1916 he sailed, after a few distracted hours of posing in a New York hotel for a portrait by Mr. F. W. Benson, which is now a treasured possession of his parents. It shows him as the aviator who, besides forming and continuing to inspire the Lafayette Escadrille, won by his own fearless service the successive ranks of sergeant, adjutant, and lieutenant, and was decorated in turn with the *Croix de Guerre* (with one star and three palms), the *Médaille Militaire,* and the *Croix de la Légion d'Honneur*, of which the last was pinned on his breast as he lay on his deathbed in the Vosges. A record of 122 aerial engagements stood to his credit — with the destruction of five German planes officially, and four others unofficially, ascribed to him.

The circumstances which brought this remarkable service to an end may best be described through a direct quotation from Mr. Babbitt's memoir:

> On the morning of Thursday, October 12 [1916], Norman and other members of his squadron were assigned to convoy a French bombarding fleet in an aerial raid on Oberndorf, a German arms and munition centre located in the Vosges near the plains of Alsace. While circling over the town, they came in close contact with a formidable array of German aircraft, and a terrific encounter ensued in which shot, shell-fire, and skillful manoeuvering disabled many of the machines on both sides. It was at the conclusion of this battle in the air that Norman's Nieuport machine struck an aerial cable while he was endeavoring to make a landing in the dark within the French lines near Luxeuil. In this collision his machine was overturned and wrecked and he was thrown violently to the ground. On being rescued by his comrades, it was found that both his legs were broken and, as was subsequently found, he had sustained a fracture of the skull. He was carried to the neighboring hospital at Gerardmer, where for a time he manifested the undaunted courage that he had always shown under adverse conditions, cheerfully requesting the attending surgeons who were setting the bones of his broken legs to

be careful not to make one shorter than the other! The skull fracture was not discovered until later, and it was as a result of this latter injury that Norman died from cerebral hemorrhage on the following Sunday morning, October 15. His comrades gathered around his bedside when he became finally unconscious, in the vain hope of detecting symptoms of renewed vitality, but he passed away peacefully as in a sleep. Those of his near relatives who had been summoned from Paris arrived at his bedside too late to find him alive.

The dead hero was given all the honors of a military funeral, which was held in the Luxeuil aviation field, where the body rested on a caisson draped with the American and French flags. The services, which were conducted by a French regimental chaplain, were attended by a large representation of the Allied military divisions, including French and English officers of high rank, as well as a full representation of the American Escadrille and pilots from the neighboring aviation camps. During the funeral, instead of the customary firing of cannon as a salutation to the dead, a squadron of aeroplanes circled in midair over the field in honor of the departed aviator, showering down myriads of flowers. The body was borne to a neighboring chapel, there to rest until the end of the war, in accordance with the military regulations governing the temporary disposition of the remains of those dying at the battle-fronts.

A memorial service, held on the following Sunday in the American Church in Paris, was described by those present as one of the most impressive ever witnessed in that sanctuary. The American colony came in full numbers to testify their admiration and appreciation of their fellow-countryman's valor and sacrifice. The President of the French Republic, the heads of the executive and legislative branches of the Government, the Army and Navy and the Diplomatic Corps were represented by their most distinguished members, and the emblems of mourning contributed to a scene that was as beautiful as it was significant and memorable.

One of his comrades in the Escadrille, J. R. McConnell, who himself was soon to fall in an air fight with the enemy, wrote to a friend, not long after Norman Prince's death, in a letter describing it, these words hitherto unpublished: "He was very brave, and sang on the way to the hospital. Poor old boy — but then, I don't think he minded going. He'd done his work and was satisfied."

EDWARD CARTER SORTWELL

Class of 1911

Edward Carter Sortwell was a native of Cambridge, of which his father, Alvin Foye Sortwell was mayor. His mother, Gertrude W. Sortwell, now a widow, is a resident of Cambridge. He was born March 25, 1889, and prepared for college at St. Paul's School, Concord, New Hampshire. He studied at Harvard for three years, leaving college, before the graduation of his class, on his father's death. He then entered the employ of the Ludlow Manufacturing Associates, and in the pursuit of this firm's transactions in jute was sent to Calcutta. Here he had been at work for three years when, in the spring of 1916, he started for home, *via* Europe. Stopping over in Paris he encountered an opportunity to join the American Ambulance Field Service, and enrolled for a term of six months. From May till September he served with Section 8 of the Service in France. Then came an opportunity to join Section 3 and go with it to Salonica; late in September he volunteered and was accepted for this duty.

In a letter written by one of Sortwell's Ambulance comrades both in France and at Salonica, Thomas B. Buffum (Harvard '16), the work of the Section, first in Champagne, then at Verdun, is described in some detail. A single passage, dealing with experiences in the Verdun neighborhood, and with Sortwell's conduct, will speak sufficiently for the nature of this service, for which his section received a citation:

From the hill above the town there was a fine view of Verdun itself and the hills around it. It was a most impressive sight that evening to watch the thousands of flashes from the guns flickering up and down the valley below us and from the hills on the other side. The next morning at dawn we each rode up to Fort Tavannes in a car of the French Ambulance Section we were replacing. This was so we could learn the road. For most of us it was our first experience under heavy shell firing. It was a pretty exciting run, but it was nothing to what we were going to get later. We crossed the river above Verdun, passed through the outskirts of the town and then up the hill on the road to Étain. This went up quite a long hill. At the top we turned off at Bellevue Farm and went through a wood to Fort Tavannes. This wood was the worst part of the run. It was always being shelled. The road was full of shell holes and lined with dead and dying horses, smashed wagons, caissons and automobiles. In the early light of dawn it was the most ghastly looking wood I have ever seen. There wasn't much shelling going on at that time in the morning except up around the Fort. There was a sort of tunnel just inside the gate where the cars stood while they were being loaded up. There was only room for three at a time, so the others had to wait way down on the side of the hill under the shelter of the bank until one of the cars had passed on the way down. Lots of times they had to wait there for hours on account of the Fort being so heavily bombarded that the cars in it could not leave. Well, that night we tried the road for ourselves for the first time. Each one of us had to make about three trips, for we were taking up the new staff for the *poste de secours* there, *brancardiers*, doctors, etc. The road was being shelled almost the whole way up, for it is at night that most of the traffic goes on. It was very dark and what with all the confusion and excitement, a lot of us got lost and fell into huge shell holes and were run down by big trucks or galloping artillery. It is certainly driving under the most trying circumstances I can think of, something like driving down Fifth Avenue on one of its most crowded days in pitch darkness, with no lights except that from bursting shells or cannon going off right in your ear, which was worse than no light at all. One of the hardest things was dodging artillery, which would come galloping on to the road from some little side road or open field. I remember coming out of the entrance to the Fort on the first trip. They were shelling the road with shrapnel and it was breaking uncomfortably near, right over head. Ed and another fellow were just ahead of me. We were empty, so we started off as fast as we could. What was our sorrow when we found a big convoy of wagons blocking the road. They were bringing up bags to the Fort and the drivers had all beat it inside until the bombardment slowed up a little. I remember that Ed was the coolest one of us. I know I was dropping down flat on the ground every time a shell would break. After a delay which seemed like hours to us, we finally got a way cleared so that we could get our cars by. When we got to Bellevue Farm we found they were shelling the cross-roads there heavily, so we had to jump out of our cars again and run down into an *abri*. It was pretty well crowded already, but we managed to squeeze in. Although very close and uncomfortable we had to stay there about a half hour while each shell seemed to land right on top of us.

When we came out we didn't expect to find anything left of our cars, but they were still there. We jumped in and just tore back the rest of the way. After the *brancardiers* had all been carried up, we returned to our scheduled morning run at dawn, which was a great relief, but on June 21 the Germans must have started an unusually big attack right on our sector. The roads were just raked with shells, and soon the wounded came pouring in. For the next four or five days we were carrying them back just as fast as we could make the trip, at all hours of the day and night, eating and sleeping whenever we could get the chance. Some of our cars were riddled with pieces of shell, one of them was almost buried by earth and stones from the explosion of a 380, but we came through with the most wonderful luck.

After Verdun there was a quieter term of service at Sommedieu, to the right of the Verdun sector. Of Sortwell's transfer to Section 3 and his journey to Salonica he wrote to his mother on November 3, 1916, when the hard journey was done:

On September 22nd when our section was near Nancy *en repos*, we had a telegram asking for volunteers to go to Salonica with another section. Ten of us sent our names in, and then we heard nothing for four days when another message came saying that myself and two others were to report in Paris. We went into Paris the next day, and I sent my cable right off to you. We expected to leave Paris in two days, but were delayed and did not get away until October 4th. I was awfully busy while in Paris buying things, working on the cars, etc. There are twenty-five Americans in this section with thirty ambulances. I knew quite a number of the men who are with us before, including Lovering Hill [Harvard, '10] who is the section leader, Charlie Baird [Harvard, '11], Graham Carey [Harvard, '14], from Cambridge, John Munroe [Harvard, '13] who went to Wiscasset once and Dan took him to Boothbay on Shada. We left Paris on the night of October 12th, for Marseilles on a train with all our cars and two passenger coaches attached. We were nearly forty hours on the way, with nothing to eat excepting what we could buy at stations on the way. We then had to wait six days there at Marseilles for a steamer. We had a great time there, went swimming every morning in the ocean, and had luncheon every day at *La Réserve*, which is the place we all went out to for tea two years ago. Had several good motor rides there also. One night I had dinner with an Englishman I used to know in Calcutta, who is now a captain in the English Army, stationed at Marseilles.

We sailed from Marseilles on October 21st on the worst old transport imaginable. There were eight hundred Indo-China troops on board, and they were the dirtiest crowd I ever hope to see. We slept in the smoke-room nights, and in the day time we had no place to go but the deck. There had been no arrangements made to feed us, but after the first day, it was arranged to give us two meals a day in the dining-room. We were eight days on that old boat, and they were about the worst eight days I have ever spent. The only good part about it was that we had good clear calm weather the whole way.

We have been here now five days, waiting for our cars, which are on another boat, to arrive. There is no word about them at all as yet, so we cannot tell how long we will be here, but as soon as we get our cars, and they are uncrated and in running order, we are to be sent right away to the front.

We are living here in tents, eight to a tent, just on the outskirts of the town. Half the section is free every day, and I am now down town writing this at a very attractive café right on the water front, where we are going to have luncheon in about an hour. It is very nice, as the street cars run very close to where our tents are.

This is a very funny place, I have never seen so many cafés in my life. The main street is all along the water front, and nearly every place on it either a café or a "movie." There are troops and officers here from about every army on the Allies' side, and you never saw such a conglomeration of uniforms in your life.

We have all signed up for seven months, starting from the 22nd September, which will get me through here the 22nd April. I do not know how soon I can get away after that, but I shall come home as soon as possible, probably arriving sometime in June, and then I want to have the summer in Wiscasset.

I was very glad of your letter, also one from M—— and one from Mrs. N——, saying that you were all glad that I had come out here, for I did not know how you would take it. I am also very sorry that I have been so long in writing you, but I will try to do better in the future.

My best love as ever,
Edward.

Eight days after writing this letter he was struck by a heavy motor car while crossing a dark street at night in Salonica. Another comrade, Charles Baird, wrote home on November 19, 1916, describing the accident and its tragic consequences:

A week ago last night Eddie Sortwell was hit by a machine while crossing the main street to get into a carriage. He hit the cobble stones hard and received a concussion. He remained unconscious till Sunday night. The doctors knew there was a clot somewhere, but as he didn't regain consciousness they couldn't operate. He died Sunday night. We buried him Wednesday morning in the French Cemetery. He had a military service and an escort of eighteen soldiers with bayonets fixed. Carey, Buffum, Armour, and Munroe were the pall-bearers. A French Protestant minister conducted the service. The automobile service was represented by a colonel and about twenty men. We were all present except five. I was to be a pall-bearer, as was Blumenthal, but only four were necessary. Eddie lies in a soldier's grave with a wooden cross over it with his name burnt in the cross piece just as the soldiers are. Eddie was working in India up until last spring when he decided to go home and see his family. *En route* he decided to join the ambulance for six months and get home this fall. Then, when his time was up, he couldn't resist coming out here with us. That meant he wouldn't get to Cambridge till next summer. And here he was, one of the nicest fellows in the section; and here he lies until the end of the war, and possibly forevermore. Covering his coffin is a French flag and also an American flag. There is a wreath with his name and an inscription, *de Section Sanitaire Américaine 3*. There are many other bunches of flowers laid there by the fellows. Eddie's death hit me hard for I liked him and he always had a glad hand for me.

To Sortwell's mother Mr. A. Piatt Andrew, Director General of the American Ambulance Field Service, wrote from Paris on November 28:

Your son has left in the memory of all of those who were associated with him, both in the section with which he first went to the front and the section to which he was transferred, as well as with us of the base staff, a fine record of arduous and in many cases dangerous work, eagerly and courageously performed; an example of manly endurance in the performance of duty which will not be forgotten. He was always ready for whatever task was assigned to him. He never hesitated and never shirked before a dangerous mission.

He is the third of our American volunteers to give his life in the service of France in her great hours of peril, and in his sacrifice he has added one more link to the bonds of friendship which have bound our two countries since their earliest days.

EDGAR ALLEN LOW SHORTT

CLASS OF 1917

BORN at Staten Island, April 17, 1896, Edward Allen Low Shortt was one of those for the day of whose death only a tentative date can be given. He was recorded "missing" December 10, 1916, and it was more than three years later that the tragic lack of further information compelled his enrolment among the "Harvard Dead."

His father, the late William Allaire Shortt, a New York lawyer, a son of an Episcopal clergyman of Irish birth, educated at the University of Dublin, and rector of parishes in the United States and Canada, was himself a graduate of Toronto University. As an undergraduate he was a sergeant in the Queen's Own Battalion of the Canadian militia, and to service with this regiment he returned when the second Riel Rebellion broke out, after his admission to the New York bar. It was through enlistment with the Canadian forces many years later that his son entered the great war.

Allen Shortt's mother was Lucy Elizabeth (Low) Shortt, a daughter of Edward Allen Low, a China merchant, of the New England family transplanted to New York and Brooklyn, and an uncle of the Hon. Seth Low. The boy was taught to speak French before he learned his native tongue, and retained a proficiency in the language which stood him in good stead when he became a soldier. The love of nature which was a marked characteristic of his youth also served a valuable purpose in the training of those powers of observation which must have helped him later to become an intelligence officer. After a trip to California when he was nine years old his father, who was his companion, reported that he must have seen "out of the back of his head," so unfailing was his perception of birds and their species.

His formal schooling was conducted at the Staten Island Academy, broken by a year of study at Rome and Cassel, Germany. In the autumn of 1913 he entered Harvard. Here, through his knowledge of languages, he became a councillor of the Cercle Français, vice-president of the Circolo Italiano, and a member of the Deutsche Verein. He was also a member of the Canadian Club. Since the age of thirteen he had been a member of the New York Fencers' Club, and at Harvard he made the fencing team. In 1914 he was also attached to the rowing squad, until incapacitated by an operation for appendicitis.

Of his war service the record that follows is taken almost *verbatim* from a statement provided by his family for the present purpose.

When war broke out in 1914, Shortt's family was in Canada, where he had spent all but three of his summers. He wished to join the army at once, but his father, judging him too young at eighteen, held him back. On his return to Harvard he enlisted in the Machine Gun Company, 8th Infantry, Massachusetts National Guard, from which he resigned in the following spring. Before his father's death in 1915 Shortt offered his services to Canada, but they were refused, for he was then in a neutral country.

In the summer of 1915, having gone, as usual, to spend his vacation in Canada, he again offered his services, claiming his grandfather's Irish birth as a qualification to fight for the Allies. He received a provisional lieutenancy, was sent to an Officers' School, and attached to the 59th Battalion, 4th Division, Canadian Expeditionary Force. Because he spoke French with fluency he was detailed to Quebec on recruiting duty. At the end of this duty he returned to his battalion at Brockville, Ontario, and shortly afterwards was married to Miss Marie Crevolin Clark, of Columbus, Ohio, in Kingston, Ontario.

Not long afterwards he received his appointment as a supernumerary, having previously only been "attached." When the Canadian War Ministry, a week later, cut off supernumeraries he requested permission to give up his rank of first lieutenant and enlist as a private in the Machine Gun Corps, so that he might go overseas with his own men. This permission was granted, and on or about April 1, 1916, he sailed for England with his organization.

In fifteen days he was made a sergeant. Measles broke out among the contingent and a number of his fellow-sergeants were taken ill. As a result he overworked, and was himself later taken ill with measles, mumps, and pneumonia at the same time.

In less than two months from the time he left Canada he received his commission as first lieutenant again, his colonel remarking upon the magnificent spirit he had shown. Granted a leave of absence owing to his illness, he became so ill at the home of a cousin in England that his wife and mother were sent for. Upon his recovery he went to France.

For gallantry in action on the Somme, October 8, 1916, he was awarded the Military Cross and made Intelligence Officer of the 58th Battalion, Third Division, Canadians. On December 10, 1916, he led a raid of forty men against the German trenches at Neuville-St. Vaast near Vimy Ridge. For this he had planned and trained the men entirely himself. After the raid, Shortt, a sergeant, and a private were reported missing. According to his superior officers, it was said that during the raid a German sprang up behind Shortt, who called out to his men, "Get him, boys," and rushed after him into an adjoining trench.

The sergeant following Shortt, and the private, were shot entering the trench. The Germans reported the sergeant as having died of wounds. The private received a head wound, was sent to a German hospital, and later repatriated. But he could furnish no information. Of Shortt nothing definite has been heard. There was a mud hole at the entrance to the trench into which he ran after the German. It was believed that he slipped and fell in the mud hole and was taken prisoner. It was reported also by prisoners taken by the battalion on the left of the 58th that an officer and non-com were taken prisoners in that trench, and that the officer had expressed himself as grateful for the treatment he had received.

It has also been reported that Shortt was sent in, by orders, without his identification disc, and that therefore he would never have given his name or other information.

HENRY RICHARD DEIGHTON SIMPSON

Class of 1918

SIMPSON'S first name was that of his father, Henry Williams Simpson, a graduate of Harvard College in the Class of 1885, a lawyer in New York City. Richard Deighton was the name of his mother's maternal grandfather, whose daughter Mrs. Doria Deighton Jones, a native of Scotland, bore an important part in the boy's education and outlook. His mother, Constance Deighton (Jones) Simpson, was, in the words of another son, the friend, constant companion, and inspiration of his whole life. He was born in New York City, January 12, 1895, had his preparation for college at private schools in and near New York, and at Eton, where he took an active part in the life of the school. His record there, his brief stay at Harvard, his military service and his death, have been described as follows by a surviving brother:

At Eton he distinguished himself at work and at play, showing particular ability at science. He was twice "Sent up for Good" (i.e., sent personally to the Headmaster for particularly excellent work) and after his first year took a "Double Remove," meaning that he did so well in examinations that he was placed ahead two forms instead of the usual one. He was good all round at sports, but especially at rowing and showed promise of becoming a notable oarsman.

Early in 1914 he took his " Little Go," the entrance examination for Cambridge University and was entered for King's College. At the beginning of August he returned to this country for the summer vacation, intending to go to Cambridge in the fall.

On the 4th of August, England went to war and Cambridge University became a hospital and training station. It was then decided that he should enter Harvard. He took up residence in Weld in September, but remained less than three weeks. The fact that his friends and companions of Eton days had answered England's call to a man and that he felt his place to be with them, fighting for the same principles and ideals of right which formed so definite a part of his character, proved too strong an appeal to be resisted. Knowing that he would have to meet strong opposition should he express his views to his family, he packed a few necessities and, having but little money on hand, took a steerage passage on a Cunarder to England, writing his mother from the pier before he sailed. His accommodations were changed by wireless, but he chose, with the captain's permission, to find out at first hand the usually unseen workings of a liner. For two days he worked with the stokers in shifts of four hours on and four hours off, later working in the engine room and other parts of the ship.

Mrs. Simpson managed to sail on a French liner the day after she received his letter and arrived in England barely in time to prevent his enlisting as a private. Very shortly a nomination for the Royal Military College at Sandhurst was obtained for him and a special Army Council called to pass on his nomination, making it possible for him to become naturalized in less than one week's time, an unprecedented thing.

At the termination of his course he was gazetted to the Sixth (Inniskilling) Dragoons as a second lieutenant. Finding that at that time the cavalry was more or less inactive, he applied to be transferred to the Royal Flying Corps. His application was approved and he was ordered to Shoreham in Sussex for preliminary training. Here he qualified and obtained his "ticket" or pilot's license. He was then transferred to Upavon in Wiltshire, for further training. From the first he showed marked ability in aviation work and this with his great enthusiasm, energy, and great-hearted wholesomeness made him a marked and trusted man among the officers and students at these stations.

In August, 1915, he received orders to go to the front and shortly was given a machine to take with him. This he accomplished by flying it to Dover and, refueling there, across the Channel to France. While over the Straits a heavy fog came up, causing him to lose direction, and, relying on instinct alone (the machine had not yet been fitted with instruments), he landed in France some miles from his objective. Finding his position, he flew on and joined his command, the Sixteenth Squadron, R.F.C., then stationed near Amiens.

On one occasion, returning from a reconnaissance behind the German line he happened to look back and saw that a comrade in another machine, the engine of which was behaving badly, was being attacked by five enemy planes. He turned back and he and his observer by their combined machine-gun fire, downed one of the Huns and drove the other four off, escorting the crippled plane to safety. His observer was badly wounded and unable to turn in his report. Consequently it was with some surprise that he learned that the observer had reported this action while in the hospital, and that as a result he himself had been mentioned in Sir John French's dispatches of January 1st, 1916, for "gallant and distinguished conduct in the field."

On a subsequent occasion his observer was again wounded and all his controls shot away. Fortunately the plane was headed for the British lines and, being a reconnaissance machine was "inherently stable." It assumed a correct gliding angle and a slight crash was the worst accident to be expected. A short distance from the ground, however, the extreme section of one of the wings collapsed and threw the machine into a dangerous side slip. By climbing out to the end of the other wing he managed to right the machine just before landing. The worst damage effected was a broken landing carriage. By some coincidence a Canadian General Staff was passing through the field he landed in, and, after his wounded observer had been carried off, he was called over to give the details of the accident to the Officer Commanding. His action had been noted with interest and some apprehension from the ground and the presence of mind that had saved the life of his observer and himself was suitably commented on. For this he was again mentioned in dispatches.

After some months' active service at the front, during which he flew almost every day, with the exception of a few weeks spent in a hospital at Boulogne recovering from injuries received in stopping the runaway horse of a comrade, he was recalled to England to conduct a series of experiments on fast fighting planes of a new type. He had previously flown the first Fokker captured intact from the enemy, and was recognized by the War Office as an expert on machines designed essentially for speed and fighting.

He later returned to the front and joined the Ninth Squadron, R.F.C., remaining there until the latter part of 1916 when he was invalided to London suffering from dysentery and general debility. While still convalescing he was asked to volunteer his services in testing a new type of plane which was calculated to prove faster than any other then in existence. He agreed to do this and on December 20, 1916, at the Joyce's Green Aerodrome, near

London, conducted the necessary tests in the presence of representatives of the Air Ministry. After putting the plane through numerous and exacting tests, during which it attained a speed of more than one hundred and forty miles per hour, he landed and reported that, although it had behaved admirably, he felt that something about it was not quite right. He decided to take it up again for further testing. Before he had reached the height of three hundred feet the plane collapsed and fell to the ground. He was mortally injured but was conscious for four hours before he took his final flight, from which there was no return. His last words showed the same fine consideration for others that he had shown throughout his life, when he said to those tending him, "Don't bother about me. I am all right."

He was buried with full military honors at Crayford in Kent.

At the time of his death he held the temporary rank of captain. In a few days more his promotion would have been confirmed.

It was his intention to return to Harvard if he survived the war. His name, marked with the asterisk distinguishing those who died in service, appeared in the Harvard Commencement programme for 1918 among the many who would naturally have been candidates for the A.B. degree at that time, "but were unable to complete their work because of their enlistment in the military or naval forces of the United States or of the Entente Allies."

HOWARD BURCHARD LINES

LL.B. 1915

LINES came to the Harvard Law School immediately upon his graduation at Dartmouth College with the Class of 1912, of which he was a popular and conspicuous member. His father, Dr. Ernest Howard Lines, now of Paris, formerly of New York, was a Dartmouth man before him.

He graduated there in 1882, and took his M.D. degree at Columbia in 1886. Elizabeth Lindsay (James) Lines, a native of Burlington, New Jersey, was the mother of their only son, born in New York, March 5, 1890.

In 1900 Dr. Lines and his family moved to Paris, where he became medical director of the New York Life Insurance Company. In Paris his son prepared for Dartmouth College at the Anglo-Saxon School. The scope of this preparation is suggested by the fact that in 1908 he passed the *baccalauréat* examination in *Latin et langues vivantes* at the Sorbonne with honorable mention. Through membership in the social organizations of Dartmouth, where, moreover, he was manager of the Gun Club, circulation manager of one publication and editor of another, and, through the persistence with which his college nickname of "Rainy" clung to him — always a friendly sign — the attractive personal qualities to which his friends bear witness are also suggested.

His legal studies at Harvard lacked a year of completion when the war began. He was then dissuaded from acting upon his immediate impulse to go to France and offer himself in her defense. In the summer of 1915, once he had gained the degree of LL.B. for which he had been working, he felt himself free, and set out at once for Paris, where in September, 1915, he volunteered for the American Ambulance Field Service, to which he was attached continuously except for a brief holiday visit to the United States in the spring of 1916, until his death in the Argonne on December 23 of that year.

After his visit to America he underwent, at Paris, an operation for appendicitis and an abdominal injury due to the lifting of heavy weights in his ambulance work, and besides, spent several weeks in hospital suffering both from chicken pox and from grippe. By September of 1916 he was able to leave Paris for the front "at the helm of a three-ton White truck" — as he wrote to a friend — "with a trailer consisting of a completely equipped field kitchen." To another friend he wrote, October 6: "Yesterday was a real day. While on a round for sick I struck a flooded road. In spots there was a foot of water and quite some considerable current. There were six of us in the car and full equipment of four soldiers — but my faith in a Ford was justified and we pulled through, though once or twice I had a terrible sinking feeling as the motor nearly died and I had to stop and kid it along. . . . Three miles of it was decidedly sufficient, but when it was over it was a most amusing experience to look back on." On November 29, Lines wrote to the same friend: "This morning one of the most peculiar things I have ever seen happened. A shell from a field gun hit a tree near the post. The shell failed to explode, but split the trunk of the tree for about half its height, went in, then turned and went a couple of feet down. At present it is perfectly visible in the middle of the trunk, the sides of which are holding it like a vise."

These letters to friends barely touch upon his personal exploits, which caused him to be recommended for the *Croix de Guerre* shortly before his death, on December 23, 1916. This was due to cerebral meningitis following acute pneumonia, and was so clearly recognized by the military authorities as the result of his ambulance work that an Army Citation of January 4, 1917, described him in these terms: "*Conducteur dévoué et courageux, évacué une première fois est revenu au front, a contracté dans le service une maladie grave et est mort pour la France.*"

A comrade in the Ambulance unit, Paul Borda Kurtz (Harvard, '16), who met his own death as an American aviator in May of 1918, wrote to his mother on Christmas Day of 1916, a letter describing the burial of Lines at La Grange aux Bois, a village in the Argonne, near Verdun, about ten miles from the trenches. The letter does not give the facts, reported elsewhere, that the *Croix de Guerre*, awarded too late for his own wearing, was pinned to his coffin, and that, besides the French flag which covered it, an American flag was folded within by Lines's comrades as a pillow for his head. This is what Paul Kurtz wrote:

Christmas, 1916.

DEAR MOTHER:

Howard Lines, who had been ill with pneumonia, died suddenly Saturday afternoon, and was buried this morning. He was as nice a boy as you could meet and was to be made *sous-chef* in a few days. Luckily his family, who live in Paris, were able to get out here for the funeral, which was quite impressive. It was raining and blowing hard when we got up this morning, but towards nine o'clock it began to clear off and for a while we had a little sunshine. One of the cars was sent off to another camp for the Protestant minister, a regular *brancardier* who was to read the service. All the officers who are connected with our service and those who are quartered in the village were present, as well as a number of men from other sections of the Ambulance who were near enough to get here.

With three others who were with the section last year I helped to carry the coffin, which was draped in the French colors and covered with flowers, from the mortuary to the doorway of the hospital where the simple services were held. We four, Dr. and Mrs. Lines and Miss Lines, stood just inside the doorway. On either side of the door were three soldiers, the guard of honor, who stood with rifles presented while the minister read the services and made a short and very appropriate speech. Outside were Mr. Andrew and former Ambassador Bacon, who had come up from Paris, all the officers and a number of soldiers, who stood with bared heads until it was over. Then we lifted the coffin and put it in the wagon which was waiting, while the body of a Russian soldier who had died the same day, was placed in another. The guard of honor accompanied the wagons with rifles carried muzzles downward, while we followed behind.

Everyone we passed on the way to the cemetery saluted or took off their hats, according to whether they were soldier or civilian, while each sentry presented arms until the procession had passed. The cemetery itself is not very large, merely a plot of ground enclosed by a rough fence and containing perhaps a hundred graves of soldiers, who have died here, each one with a black wooden cross with the name, regiment, and date of death painted in white letters, and on each a *couronne* of flowers. We four lifted the coffin from the wagon and carried it to the edge of the grave. There was another short address by the minister and it was all over.

A Dartmouth Bed was established in Lines's memory at the American Ambulance Hospital in Paris; a *Médaille Commemorative* of France does him further honor. This decoration was bestowed also upon his father, Dr. Lines, in 1917, and in 1918 he was made a Chevalier of the Legion of Honor in recognition of his work at Quai Debilly School for the reëducation of French maimed soldiers.

LORD GORELL
(HENRY GORELL BARNES)

LAW 1903–04

WHEN Henry Gorell Barnes, of London, attended the Harvard Law School in the academic year, 1903–04, his father, Ronald Gorell Barnes, an eminent British judge, President of the Probate, Divorce, and Admiralty Division, had not yet been raised to the peerage. In 1909 he became Baron Gorell. His eldest son, the subject of this memoir, succeeded to the title in 1913.

He was born in London, January 21, 1882. His mother was Mary Humpston (Mitchell) Barnes. He was educated at Winchester and Trinity College, Oxford, where he received the degree of B.A. in 1903, and M.A. in 1908, and at Harvard. Here he became a member of the Kalumet Club and of the University cricket team. Both in his profession of the law and as a member of the House of Lords he gave proof of talents of a high order. Two books, "The Divorce Commission" and "The Reports Summarized" (prepared with a collaborator), bear his name as author. In his private life he was greatly interested in Masonry, and for one year was Junior Grand Warden of England; before the war, also, he was chairman of the Kensington Division of the British Red Cross Society.

His record in war was as creditable as in peace. When he fell in action near Ypres, January 16, 1917, he had seen twenty-two months of continuous service in France and Belgium. He was then major of the 9th Battery, 7th London Brigade, 47th (London) Division of the British Army. On November of 1916, he was gazetted for the Distinguished Service Order for valor described in the following terms: "he pushed forward and handled his battery under very heavy fire with the greatest courage and skill. Later he carried out a daring reconnaissance and obtained most valuable information." The regard in which he was held in England may be inferred from the fact that shortly before his death he was chosen to second the King's speech at the opening of the House of Lords — a ceremony in which he did not live to participate.

Of the manner of Lord Gorell's death, reported more minutely to have occurred at the Railway Cutting between his battery position at Lankhof Farm and the front nearby, his uncle has written:

It was at Lankhof Farm, twenty-five hundred yards south of Ypres, that he was struck by a shell. He was taken to a hospital at Poperinghe and died in a few hours. I was in that part of the country last summer and met several of the men of Henry's regiment, and took down what they said of him. All united in saying that he was a splendid officer, and that the men would have followed him anywhere. He plainly inspired deep affection. He was buried in the cemetery near the C. C. S. between Poperinghe and Steenwoorde, and we had a great and splendid cross made of great oak beams from the cloisters of Ypres Cathedral erected over his grave.

To these words should be added the tributes of two friends. The first, from "J. M." appeared in the London *Times* for January 19, 1917.

I knew Lord Gorell well, and to know him was to love him. He was endowed with many of the qualities, and among them sagacity, penetration, and thoroughness, which made his father one of the foremost judges of his generation. But he had also gifts all his own which endeared him to many and which seemed to ensure a career of distinction. In all that he touched — and in his short life that was much — he succeeded, and always with ease. His work as secretary of the Divorce Commission revealed his business capacity, and in the preparation of the memorable Report of the Majority his father was greatly assisted by him. He had already obtained considerable practice at the Bar when, on succeeding to the peerage, he left the legal profession. In the House of Lords his speeches were much commended, and he proved a very effective member of the Parliamentary Committees on which he served. In illustration of his many-sided activity, it may be mentioned that he took a keen interest in Masonry, and that last year he was Junior Grand Warden of England.

Lord Gorell's interest in the Territorial scheme from the outset was great. In March, 1915, he took the battery of which he was in command to the front, and he remained in command of it until his death. His duties as an officer were performed with that thoroughness which marked all that he did.

His many friends will regret that a career rich in promise has been cut short. They will think often of the loss of a bright, simple, and strong spirit, of one who did his duty, whatever it might be, with a certain grace and winning gaiety, with modesty and alacrity. Only a few weeks ago when home on leave for some days — he had been abroad continuously for nearly two years — he spoke of the "mystery" of the struggle in which so many of his friends had fallen, but with calm assurance as to what it was for him to do. Among the many, duty-loving and faithful, whom the insatiable battlefield keeps, none will be missed more than he.

The second was from a Harvard friend, Major Francis T. Colby, U.S.A., of the Class of 1905, serving as lieutenant in the 13th Belgian Field Artillery, B.E.F., at the time his tribute to Lord Gorell appeared in the *Harvard Alumni Bulletin* of March 29, 1917:

Harvard has lost another of her sons and one of the noblest of her race: Major Lord Gorell, D.S.O., was killed in action on January 16. He fell after two years of war, commanding the same battery that he commanded at the outbreak of hostilities.

The friends whom he made at Harvard are many and lifelong, as was the warmhearted friendship which he gave to them in return. Those of us who knew and loved him as Henry Gorell Barnes during his life at the University will remember him with a clearness which the years cannot alter. His warm, highly refined, and unselfish personality made him at once our friend, although he came to Harvard a foreigner from our mother-country, while his splendid character commanded our respect. He showed even then above all other qualities the power and vigorous energy of his mind, which later enabled him to rise with such rapidity in his profession of the law, to serve with such well recognized efficiency as his father's secretary on the Royal Divorce Commission and in other executive and legal positions of importance. When, after his father's death, he took his place on the Cross Benches of the House of Lords as a Peer of England, his marked abilities and earnest application quickly gained for him the respect of the House, and it became clear that in him was to be found one of the future men of the Empire.

To those of us who have known him in France and Belgium during the past two years of war another side of his remarkable personality was shown. His highly trained judicial mind was applied to the soldier's profession, and with it was coupled the man of action and of tireless physical energy. He combined strangely the many, often conflicting, qualities which make up a good battery commander. His battery was splendidly organized, trained, and disciplined, and he was intensely loved by his officers and men. He was an excellent horseman and horsemaster. His fire was delivered with speed and accuracy, and his gun positions were always carefully prepared. The day before his death he showed me a nearly invisible gunpit which had resisted two direct hits.

He was decorated with the Distinguished Service Order for a most daring and highly successful reconnaissance between the hostile lines at the battle of the Somme.

As we carried him on our shoulders to his last resting place in a foreign land, for whose defense he had given his life, and buried him with full military honors, we felt that his loss was not the least of England's sacrifices.

ADDISON LEECH BLISS

CLASS OF 1914

THE war record of Addison Leech Bliss is extremely brief. Early in January, 1917, he resigned a business position in Pittsburgh to enter the American Ambulance Field Service. He sailed for France January 27. Immediately on reaching Paris, after a stormy voyage, he contracted a cold from which pneumonia developed. He was taken to the American Hospital at Neuilly, and there died February 22, 1917, less than a month after taking ship from the United States.

His father was Chester William Bliss, of Boston, a member of the Harvard Class of 1884, a son of William Bliss and Margaret (Chapin) Bliss, of Springfield, Massachusetts. His mother was Isadora (Leech) Bliss, a native of Leechborough, Pennsylvania. Their son, the subject of this memoir, was born in Springfield, November 21, 1891. From early schooling in Springfield, he passed to the Fay School and St. Mark's at Southborough, Massachusetts. At St. Mark's he was captain of the football team in his sixth form year, and at Harvard, which he entered in the autumn of 1910, was a member of the freshman eleven. Here, too, he belonged to the Institute of 1770, the Hasty Pudding, Sphinx, and Polo Clubs. His second undergraduate year was passed at Haverford College, his third entirely at Harvard; at Christmas of his fourth year he left college and entered the employ of the Ellsworth Collieries Company, at Ellsworth, Pennsylvania, and then of the Union Collieries Company, of Pittsburgh. Of this company he was a director, concerned especially with installation work. From this employment he went direct to France, and his death.

Between the lines of this short story much may be read in the light of two sentences found in the Class Report of 1914 next following his death: "There was no member of the Class of 1914 whose loss would be more deeply grieved. His generosity, geniality, and whole-heartedness made him one of the most lovable men it is given us to know."

HENRY MONTGOMERY SUCKLEY

CLASS OF 1910

SUCKLEY was named for his grandfather, the Rev. Dr. Henry Eglinton Montgomery, second rector of the Church of the Incarnation, New York City. At a service in memory of Henry Suckley the present rector of Dr. Montgomery's parish defined his predecessor as a man of unbounded vitality, of quick and impulsive sympathy, of ardent patriotism, and possessed of a very genius for friendship; and went on to say: "it is natural to look for these traits in his grandson, and take satisfaction in seeing their interplay in the formation of a new character."

The boy was born in Orange, New Jersey, February 18, 1887, the son of Robert Bowne Suckley, and Elizabeth (Montgomery) Suckley of Rhinebeck, New York. Here on the Hudson and at schools in Switzerland and Germany, Suckley was prepared for the one year of special preparation to enter Harvard which he received at Phillips-Exeter Academy. From 1906 to 1910, when he took his A.B. degree, he was a student at Cambridge. Here he played on the soccer football team, and belonged to the Cercle Français, and the Aero, Freshman Debating, Institute, D.K.E., Hasty Pudding, and Zeta Psi Clubs. On graduating from college he travelled in Europe, and then entered business in New York, where he was at work when the war came.

He must be counted among the Americans who gave the earliest heed to the call from Europe, for he was one of the thirty-three college men who sailed with Mr. A. Piatt Andrew in November of 1914 to enter the American Ambulance Field Service. Through the ensuing winter he served with Section 3 of that service, in the Vosges Mountains, driving an ambulance provided by St. Paul's School. "His letters to the school," said the Rev. Howard C. Robbins in the address already quoted, "afforded unconsciously an insight into his character. He is continually expressing solicitude for the wounded men under his care. Every jolt over the rough roads is, he knows, anguish to them, and his letters show how lively his sympathies were, and how assiduous his care." During the German attack in the Vosges his bravery in action won him the *Croix de Guerre* and promotion to *sous-lieutenant* under his classmate, Lovering Hill. Holding this rank he served with Section 3 at Malzeville, Verdun, and Pont-à-Mousson, and constantly distinguished himself by executive ability and coolness under shell-fire. The citation he received while in the Vosges testified to his qualities in the following terms:

Citation à la 66ème Division

Le Conducteur SUCKLEY, H., de la Section Sanitaire Américaine No. 2, sujet Américain:

A de nouveau fait preuve d'un dévouement digne des plus grands éloges en assurant nuit et jour, pendant quinze jours, avec un parfait mépris du danger, l'évacuation de nombreux blessés sur une route de montagne constamment battue par des projectiles ennemis.

In September of 1916 he returned to America to recruit and organize a new section for the Ambulance Field Service, for which his uncle, Mr. Henry Montgomery of New York, secured from members of the New York Stock Exchange the funds required for twenty new ambulances. When he returned to France in November this unit was placed under his command and ordered to Salonica. Here he served until his death, March 19, 1917, from the effects of bombing by an enemy airplane. His conduct on this front had caused General Sarrail to propose him, before his death, for the Legion of Honor, and won from an official of the Field Service the statement that "of the many hundred Americans who have come and gone in this service during the past two years, he was one of the three or four on whom we most depended, and who was most liked and trusted by those who worked with him and for him."

The circumstances of his death at Koritza in Albania on March 19 from wounds received the previous day at Zemlak, nearby, are related in a letter from Gordon Ware (Harvard, '08), whose account of the capture of the aviator responsible for Suckley's death must be given for its picture of the conditions under which our ambulance men were working:

On March 18 came the news that Henry Suckley, our chef, had been hit by an avion, and on the 19th he died in the hospital at K. It took place at Z., our former camp forty kilos from here, where he had gone to see about some supplies, etc. They were in the dining-tent at one o'clock, Henry and R. Outside was W. cleaning his car. At the first explosion Henry went outside to investigate, and the second bomb struck him, shattering his hip. R. threw himself flat and escaped injury. Henry lay there smiling and said in French: "I am hit." "*Je suis touché aussi,*" said the lieutenant's chauffeur, who had received a slight wound. An Albanian and a Frenchman were killed outright, the kitchen was riddled, and the cook wounded in the leg. Pieces of *éclat* went into W.'s car, missing him. D. had his wrist scratched and S. had a hole in his coat. Two more bombs fell near our unoccupied sleeping tent.

W. cranked up his car and took Henry, smiling and smoking, to K. "If I'm going to pass out, I'll have a cigarette first," he said, the calmest of the lot. The lieutenant's chauffeur, who is the butt of every one, proved himself a real hero and refused aid and transportation until Henry had been attended to. At K. everything possible was done for him, but only his strong constitution enabled him to last the night, an artery having been severed. He suffered little and was always conscious, not realizing until the end that he was going. Bright and cheerful, even the doctor broke down when he went. It gives an idea of the man's charm that he could so grip strangers, and it is difficult to measure our regard for him after three months' close association. As a section-leader he worked like a dog, and asked nothing of anyone which he would not do himself. The hardest thing is that he must go before the section can make or break itself. The Legion of Honor was wired him.

Henry was buried at K. on the 20th. Duty kept me here, and I'm glad. I prefer that my last impression of him should be the short talk we had on the day of his death when I passed him on the road. In the evening I took the parson who conducted the funeral back to the advanced post. He was a thoroughbred. Being the only Protestant hereabouts — a Frenchman — he had come down on horseback from the first line of trenches and offered his services. He described the funeral at which the French accorded our dead every honor. . . .

Early this morning, the Boche avion appeared — the one which killed Suckley — and about eleven it was sighted flying low over the mountains to the east. In fact he was very low, and down the road came the snap of rifle-fire as they took pot-shots at him. Nearer and nearer he flew, following the road; so it seemed that it must be his object to *mitrailleuse* the camp. Following orders, we were heading for the *abris*, when it became perfectly evident that he must be in trouble. He was not more than one hundred feet up and descending every minute, as if in search of a landing-place. It could not be otherwise, as he was too good a target for the rifle-fire. Four hundred yards from us he chose a field, swooped down — apparently always in perfect control of his machine — till, at the moment of alighting, a sharp turn of the wheel capsized her and she lay on her side, the black crosses on her belly staring at us. The rush to the *abris* stopped and the race to the machine, which was blazing briskly, began. The recollection of our own tragedy was too fresh to make us wish anything but harm to the occupants, and it was more like a Southern lynching mob than a Red Cross section that streamed over the field in the van of a thousand Frenchmen yelling with joy at the plight of the avion.

It wasn't pretty, but to give what credit can be given, I think we were all relieved to see the two men emerge more frightened than hurt and approach the on-coming mob with raised hands, crying, "Kamerad, Kamerad." They were instantly surrounded by a jostling throng, more curious than ugly, though it was necessary for them to appeal to a French officer to stop the soldiers from cutting off their buttons as souvenirs. As the officers seemed inclined to do little, I'm glad to say it was an American who finally shamed the mob into letting them alone—and I hope this will be scored to the credit of our own memento-seeking tourists. The men were white and frightened, uncertain as to their reception. As their French was not good they could hardly have been reassured by a lieutenant's threat to shoot them — emphasizing the point with drawn revolver — should their denial that there were bombs in the machine prove false. The officer was a good-looking young chap with a keen, American-like face. His non-com was of the caricatured Prussian type, bull-necked, bullet-headed, and brutal in appearance. The officer had three decorations, including the inevitable Iron Cross. "*Le moteur est — est — en panne*," he said hesitatingly, and claimed that it had been going badly all the morning and at length, catching fire, had forced his descent, accidentally unsuccessful. I think he deliberately capsized it so as to destroy it.

Meanwhile the burning machine was given a wide berth by the crowd, as the fire had reached the ammunition and constant crackling of cartridges resulted. Half a dozen signal-rockets likewise exploded in a half-hearted manner. The camera fiends were the first to enter the danger zone, and the ruins were still smouldering when the souvenir hunters swooped down like Albanians on a dead horse. I found myself in a tug-of-war with a *Chasseur d'Afrique* for a bit of canvas with the black cross on it. He won. In an incredibly short time fire and scavengers had left nothing but the big motor standing. The prisoners were marched off to headquarters. They were the pair who had killed Henry Suckley.[1]

[1] *Harvard Alumni Bulletin*, May 24, 1917.

PRINTED AT
THE HARVARD UNIVERSITY PRESS
CAMBRIDGE, MASS., U.S.A.

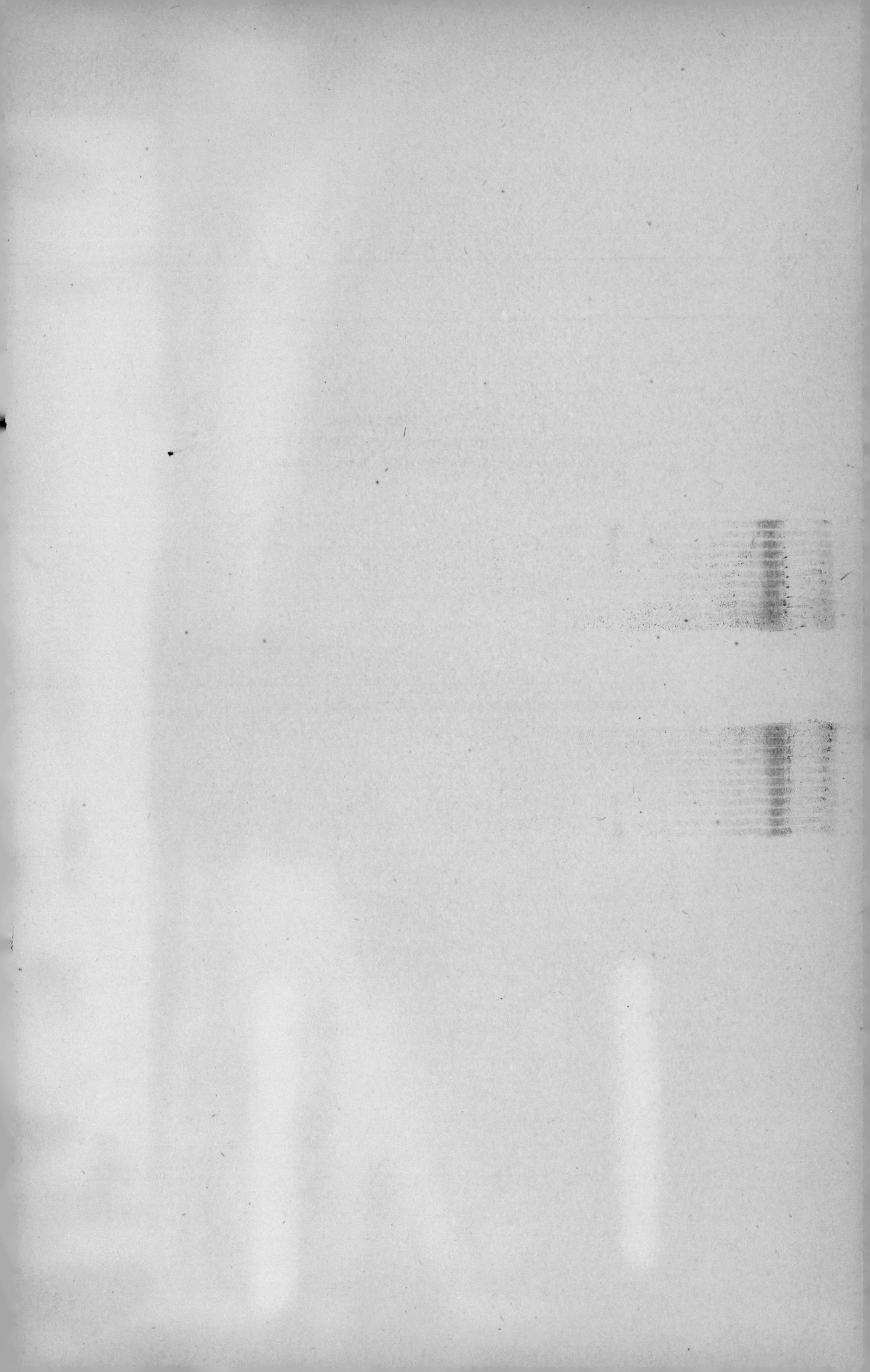

Memoirs of the Harvard dead V. I.